The Student-Centered *Classroom*

Transforming Your

Teaching and

Grading Practices

JEANETTA JONES MILLER

Solution Tree | Press

Copyright © 2021 by Solution Tree Press

Materials appearing here are copyrighted. With one exception, all rights are reserved. Readers may reproduce only those pages marked "Reproducible." Otherwise, no part of this book may be reproduced or transmitted in any form or by any means (electronic, photocopying, recording, or otherwise) without prior written permission of the publisher.

555 North Morton Street
Bloomington, IN 47404
800.733.6786 (toll free) / 812.336.7700
FAX: 812.336.7790

email: info@SolutionTree.com
SolutionTree.com

Visit **go.SolutionTree.com/instruction** to download the free reproducibles in this book.

Printed in the United States of America

Library of Congress Cataloging-in-Publication Data

Names: Miller, Jeanetta Jones, author.
Title: The student-centered classroom : transforming your teaching and
   grading practices / Jeanetta Jones Miller.
Description: Bloomington, IN : Solution Tree Press, [2020] | Includes
   bibliographical references and index.
Identifiers: LCCN 2020014332 (print) | LCCN 2020014333 (ebook) | ISBN
   9781949539998 (paperback) | ISBN 9781947604834 (ebook)
Subjects: LCSH: Student-centered learning. | Grading and marking (Students)
   | Teacher effectiveness. | Motivation in education.
Classification: LCC LB1027.23 .M55 2020 (print) | LCC LB1027.23 (ebook) |
   DDC 371.3--dc23
LC record available at https://lccn.loc.gov/2020014332
LC ebook record available at https://lccn.loc.gov/2020014333

Solution Tree
Jeffrey C. Jones, CEO
Edmund M. Ackerman, President

Solution Tree Press
President and Publisher: Douglas M. Rife
Associate Publisher: Sarah Payne-Mills
Art Director: Rian Anderson
Managing Production Editor: Kendra Slayton
Production Editor: Miranda Addonizio
Content Development Specialist: Amy Rubenstein
Copy Editor: Evie Madsen
Proofreader: Sarah Ludwig
Text and Cover Designer: Laura Cox
Editorial Assistants: Sarah Ludwig and Elijah Oates

Acknowledgments

I am grateful to the students who put up with my early attempts to make my classroom student centered, and I owe many thanks to the students who came later and were willing to work with me to profoundly change the focus of the classroom so they shared responsibility with me and with one another for the quality of their learning.

I also want to thank the Solution Tree team for its high standards and encouraging, supportive approach and to express my gratitude to Amy Rubenstein and Miranda Addonizio, who know how to ask the hard questions and, also, when to offer insightful comments and suggestions.

Solution Tree Press would like to thank the following reviewers:

Aaron Blackwelder
Founder of Teachers Going Gradeless
English Teacher
Woodland High School
Woodland, Washington

Katie Heavlin
Assistant Principal
Roosevelt High School
Sioux Falls, South Dakota

Kathleen Mills
English Teacher
Bloomington High School South
Bloomington, Indiana

Kate Miner
Instructional Coach
Shawnee Mission North High School
Overland Park, Kansas

Shauna Petersen
First-Grade Teacher
Moore Elementary School
Des Moines, Iowa

Lindsay Yearta
Assistant Professor of Education
Winthrop University
Rock Hill, South Carolina

Megan Youngkent
Instructional Coach
Cedar Falls High School
Cedar Falls, Iowa

Visit **go.SolutionTree.com/instruction** to download the free reproducibles in this book.

Table of Contents

Reproducible pages are in italics.

About the Author vii

Introduction 1

Chapter 1: Encourage Academic Success 11
Integration With Student Interests 11
Interaction Among Students 13
Individualization to Ensure Students Feel Known and Respected . . . 24
Next Steps for Encouraging Academic Success 25

Chapter 2: Support Personal Growth 27
Independent Thinking 28
Imaginative Freedom 31
Integrity 34
Next Steps for Supporting Personal Growth 38

Chapter 3: Make Space for Speaking and Listening 39
Speech to Facilitate Thought 40
Enhanced Listening Through Writing and Speaking 48
Next Steps for Making Space for Speaking and Listening 58

Chapter 4: Deepen Understanding With Writing
and Reading 61
Achievement of Multiple Purposes With Writing 62
Illumination of the Process of Reading 80
Next Steps for Deepening Understanding With Writing
and Reading 88

Chapter 5: Meet Individual Needs in the Evaluation Process ... 89
  The Problems With Traditional Grading Systems 89
  The Promise of the Student-Centered Approach 94
  Next Steps for Meeting Individual Needs in the Evaluation Process .118

Chapter 6: Communicate With the School Community 119
  Communication With Colleagues 120
  Communication With Administrators 122
  Communication With Parents 124
  Next Steps for Communicating With the School Community *127*

Epilogue: Conclusion 129

Appendix: Frequently Asked Questions 131

References and Resources 139

Index 147

About the Author

Jeanetta Jones Miller has been an educator since 1986. Her education experiences range from California to Connecticut and from working with continuation high school students in a voluntary diploma program and integrating all subject areas with fifth graders to taking a student-centered approach in high school. She has taught American studies and senior projects as well as a variety of English courses. Miller has served as department chair and mentored many teachers with a consistent focus on research, development, and implementation of strategies that help all students engage deeply in learning.

Miller has participated in a number of organizations related to her teaching and leadership goals, including the National Council of Teachers of English (NCTE) and the Connecticut Writing Project. She served on district committees that studied graduation standards, K–12 language arts, and aspects of learning such as reflection and self-direction. She was a lead writer for Newtown High School's (Connecticut) successful application for recognition as a U.S. Department of Education Blue Ribbon School in 2000. In 2010, she won NCTE's English Language Arts Teacher Educators (ELATE) James Moffett Memorial Award for teacher research. Miller's conviction is that individual classroom teachers can take a student-centered approach to teaching and evaluation within a traditional school culture. She further developed this belief in a 2013 article for *English Journal* that serves as a resource for professional development programs. Miller has also contributed to *California English*. With two colleagues, she wrote *High Stakes High School*, a publication designed to help parents navigate standardized testing.

Miller earned a bachelor's degree from Mills College and qualified for both multiple- and single-subject teaching credentials at California State University, East Bay. She earned a master's degree in education from Western Connecticut State University and an intermediate administrator's certificate from Sacred Heart University.

To book Jeanetta Jones Miller for professional development, contact pd@SolutionTree.com.

Introduction

I was shocked speechless when I first heard the old teacher joke about grading papers using the "staircase distribution" method. If you've been spared this joke so far, the idea is that the teacher grades a stack of papers by tossing them down a staircase. The papers that land at the bottom are presumed to be the heaviest and, therefore, the best. They get As. The "lightweights" that stay on top get Ds. The "in-betweens" get Bs and Cs.

Like any joke that hangs around year after year, there is a nugget of truth to this one. I knew some veteran teachers size up and label students: B student, C student, and so on. One of the teachers in the English department at the high school where I'd recently been hired told me it was the responsibility of teachers to sort students for the state university system. So, I was amazed to learn someone was coming to the high school to conduct professional development sessions with teachers about the idea that every student can be an A student.

Our professional development presenter, Harvey Silver, challenged the idea that grades should always fall neatly along a bell curve—or staircase—and urged us to see each student as a unique individual rather than as a B or a C. He was an engaging presenter—down-to-earth, funny, inspiring, with a big reassuring presence. His approach seemed easy-going, but he was on a research mission to help teachers apply theories about multiple intelligences and learning styles in the classroom. His work would lead to the publication of *So Each May Learn* (Silver, Strong, & Perini, 2000) and many more books with the purpose of giving teachers tools to focus on how students learn. I was convinced by his presentation and ready to give *As for all* a try.

I designed menus of assignment options students could choose from based on learning style and personal interests. The students produced amazing work. I still have a painting one student did of Doc from John Steinbeck's (1945) novel

Cannery Row gazing out over Monterey Bay. We had a wonderful time, and lots of students earned lots of As.

Then, I heard there was going to be a special faculty meeting and wondered what it would be about. It turned out we assembled to study grade distribution among faculty members. The percentage of As was remarkably consistent except for two of us. No names were mentioned, but everyone knew the two teachers were the two new hires—myself and another teacher who must have found Silver's ideas as enthralling as I did. Senior faculty members spoke about how important it was for students and, of course, the university system to perceive all of the school's programs and courses as rigorous. They were confident the grading anomaly would not happen again. Meeting adjourned.

Reeling, I went home to cry on my husband's shoulder. The next day I came home to a dozen roses and a card that read, "Honey, I don't think you're easy." The roses faded, but I still have the card. At this point, I'd taught for about five years, but this was my first job in a traditional high school. The meeting about grades made it clear that the vast majority of the faculty saw Silver's visit as just another professional development program to ignore. Colleagues assured me that these sorts of fads tend to come and go. I didn't agree, but I realized that I would probably be more successful at doing something new if I had earned some credibility doing what everyone else did. I kept my head (and the number of As) down and, for a while, tried to become a good sorter of students for the university system.

I tell this personal story because I'm guessing there are a lot of teachers with experiences similar to my own. Silver's visit took place in the early 1990s. Yet the question he raised has been taken up by others, and is still being asked, such as by education author Alfie Kohn (2019b) in an article for *The New York Times* called "Why Can't Everyone Get A's?"

The traditional system says that if everyone gets an A, it doesn't mean teachers and students are doing a great job. It simply means the standards aren't high enough. According to Kohn (2019b):

> Its inspiring rhetoric notwithstanding, the standards-and-accountability movement is not about universal improvement or leaving no child behind. To the contrary, it is an elaborate sorting device, intended to separate wheat from chaff. The fact that students of color, students from low-income families, and students whose first language isn't English are disproportionately defined as chaff makes the whole enterprise even more insidious. . . . Excellence has been defined—for ideological reasons—as something that can't be achieved by everyone.

Taking the student-centered approach to teaching and evaluation this book describes creates a playing field where the game is not rigged. This approach invites students to work collaboratively to make progress toward achievement of learning goals. Students need not compete with one another to experience success. As Kohn (2019b) points out, "Indeed, a surprisingly consistent body of social science evidence shows that competition tends to hold us back from doing our best—particularly in comparison with cooperation, in which people work with, not against, each other." Traditional school culture is hard to change because it is part of a larger culture accustomed to distributing individuals just like tossing papers down a staircase, with many bunched precariously at the top and few securely landing at the bottom. But change is possible when teachers, who have come to believe this system is unfair to students, have the courage to set up student-centered classrooms within the traditional school.

Teacher by teacher, classroom by classroom, taking a student-centered approach can have an immediate positive impact on students and, over time, build their skills and confidence to help them become active members of their communities. For example, the Stanford Center for Opportunity Policy in Education (SCOPE) conducted its Student-Centered Schools Study at four Northern California schools (McKenna, 2014). Barbara McKenna (2014) of SCOPE reports findings that show, initially, a student-centered approach helps students "feel a sense of purpose and connection to school." In the long term, SCOPE faculty director Linda Darling-Hammond concludes, "The numbers are compelling . . . students in the study schools exhibited greater gains in achievement than their peers, had higher graduation rates, were better prepared for college, and showed greater persistence in college" (as cited in McKenna, 2014). Students can and should expect their schools to do more than sort them. As Kohn (2019b) says, "Perhaps it's time to rescue the essence of excellence—a more common-sense understanding of the idea that is also more democratic: Everyone may not get there, but at least in theory all of us could."

Instead of sorting students, teachers must provide the most *likely conditions* in which they can work together. During the winter of 1999, I participated in a project that joined high school students and fourth graders. The idea was to cross lines between buildings and grade levels in preparation for a visit from Ruby Bridges Hall, who, as a six-year-old in 1960, crossed one of the hardest lines of all by walking up the steps of the all-White William Frantz Elementary School to start first grade. After studying Norman Rockwell's (1964) well-known painting of the small Black girl in her white dress with four U.S. marshals surrounding her, the students responded with poetry and drawings. We watched the Disney TV movie *Ruby Bridges* (Hopkins & Palcy, 1998) and talked about how hard it had been on Ruby and her family to put themselves on that line. When Ms. Hall came to speak with us, the high school auditorium was full because the entire junior class also attended. Ms. Hall seemed almost as small at the front of that auditorium as she seemed next to the tall marshals in the painting, and her voice was quiet when she spoke, but it was the only sound in that big room because everyone was listening so intently. In her autobiography, Ms. Hall writes, "If kids from different races are to grow up to live and work together in harmony, then they are going to have to begin at the beginning—in school together" (Bridges, 1999, p. 58).

The ultimate purpose of the student-centered teaching practices this book describes is to make it possible for school to fulfill its best and most enduring promise: to give each student a fair chance to grow up literate, with an open mind, and with an intact interest in being an active citizen and community member. There's no need for a line between school and the larger world. What's urgent in the larger world is urgent in the classroom. What students learn in the classroom about who they are and what they want from life can make it possible for them to speak out in the larger world to those who perpetuate the prejudices that have held us back for too long.

The student-centered approach makes it possible for the teacher to take on the role of guide and mentor—the caring adult every child needs as many of as possible—right there in the classroom. Traditional teaching methods raise barriers between teacher and student in the form of one-size-fits-all lessons, tests, and grades that put students in their place and keep them there.

In an article for *Education Week*, Kohn (2019a) writes:

> One of the most important lessons I've learned in my career is that the best way to respond to a question is not always to offer an answer. Sometimes one should linger on the question itself, asking what assumptions it conceals and what other questions it displaces. Many questions in education, for example, take for granted the inevitability of traditional practices.

Instead of asking what knowledge and skills students must acquire, teachers need to ask themselves, "Why should we impose a preordained curriculum on students instead of working with them to determine what they actually need and want?" According to Kohn (2019a):

> [That] requires not only relinquishing some control but learning more about students' interests and how to involve them in figuring out which topics to pursue and how best to do so. The same is true of solving tricky discipline problems, or deciding how to arrange and decorate the classroom. A teacher who simply wonders whether (or when or how) to do x isn't asking the far more consequential question.

The question is not *what* should be in the curriculum, but *how* teachers can make the curriculum flexible and responsive to real students and real needs. The answer is attention to contemporary issues and interests; recognition of the unique experiences each student brings to the classroom; focus on the essential, but seldom-tested, skills of speaking and listening; writing as an integral component of a life that is both active and reflective; access to reading as a source of information and pleasure; timely and specific feedback on work in progress; and experience working in partnerships with others. Even elementary students are aware of themselves as learners with preferences for one modality over others, and interests that can open doors to new knowledge and skills. Even elementary students enter the classroom with some experience of the larger world and some expectations about how teachers will treat them and how they ought to treat others. And for secondary students who have already spent many years in a variety of classrooms, the need for relevance and meaning is intense. The student-centered classroom provides both.

Big ideas and lofty goals are inspiring, but they can also be overwhelming. You may be wondering how in the world individual teachers can make a difference. And that's why I wrote this book. In the following chapters, I concentrate on what you can do in your classroom to effect positive change for your students.

The first inklings of these ideas started for me even before I became a teacher. I used to volunteer in my older son's first-grade class. Mostly the teacher asked me to sit with reading groups, but one day she asked me to stay with a student named Lamar because she wanted him to finish his mathematics worksheet before going to lunch. The worksheet had Lamar in tears. He wanted so much to be at lunch with the other students. It seemed all wrong, but the teacher had a good reputation, and, surely, she knew what was appropriate for the student. This situation made me want to know more about education theory, which launched me into a midlife career change. After I earned teacher certification, I worked in the district where my older son attended elementary school, starting with a session of summer school and then spending two years each at an alternative high school and an elementary school. The alternative high school was what is known as a continuation high school, which helps older students earn a high school diploma.

The continuation high school gave me an opportunity early in my teaching career to work with students who had not been successful in a traditional school setting. Most of the students I worked with had lost a year or more of school to drugs or family issues. About half the students dropped out sometime during the first semester, which was not unusual; part of the role that alternative schools play is to reduce the number of students who would drop out if they were still in the mainstream school setting, but it remains a challenge to keep students in school when they are not accustomed to success. The other half persevered and, usually after two years in the program, earned their diplomas.

Because many of the students had jobs, the program met in the morning, from 8 a.m. to noon, with a 10 a.m. break in the middle. There were two teachers. I was responsible for teaching art, English, and social studies. I had half of the students from 8 a.m. to the break, while the other teacher taught computer literacy, mathematics, and science. Then we switched students for the second portion of the morning. Because time was short, the other teacher and I tried to build opportunities to develop a variety of skills into every assignment, and we tried to focus each assignment on concepts that matter to students. Over the course of two years, I got to know the students well and learned so much from them. There were only a few graduates at the end of my first year with the program, but as I got better at meeting the students where they were and building on their interests, their ability to take responsibility for their own education surged, and the number of graduates at the end of that second year underscored the positive impact of taking a student-centered approach. The district's records showed their failures, but the students knew somehow the system had failed them too. However, in a setting where the teachers knew and respected them, these students were able to overcome the past and move forward.

The fifth-grade classrooms in the elementary school where I taught next were organized in clusters, with four classrooms surrounding an inner room where teachers could share resources. It was easy to bring two or more classes together for a special event. The students went out for music and physical education, but the teachers could design the rest of the day to tailor it to the needs and interests of each class. Bells did not ring every fifty minutes. We could integrate science and mathematics with a history activity focused on pioneers preparing to cross the country in covered wagons. Students could choose their own books from the classroom library, listen to books read aloud, and read books in partnership with other students. The learning environment was supportive and stimulating.

I ran into Lamar again when I was a newly fledged fifth-grade teacher. Lamar had grown into a tall, quiet boy who did what was asked of him—"a good soldier," as one of my continuation high school students liked to describe himself. He, like many other students, marched steadily through school doing what he was told—no more, no less—because he had figured out that trying to do things his way or have a say in what goes on in the classroom takes a lot of time and energy and could even get him in trouble. I wanted to see Lamar really engaged in learning and got lucky with a mathematics project. I invited students to use what they were learning about geometric shapes to design and model a building they could live, play, work, retreat in—whatever their current dream of the future might suggest. Lamar lit up, and I heard excitement in his voice for the first time.

Although the ages and backgrounds of the students were so different, in both continuation high school and elementary school, it was natural to take a student-centered approach. These experiences stayed with me when I began to work in the district's mainstream high school. I read books and attended conferences, hoping to learn more. From John Dewey (1900, 1990) to Alfie Kohn (2019a, 2019b), from James Moffett (1994) to Deborah Meier (Gasoi & Meier, 2018), there is a lot of passionate advocacy for a student-centered approach, especially for students who struggle to meet academic goals.

I wanted mainstream high school to be more like the continuation high school and elementary schools where I had taught. Listening to me fret over having to assign the same novel to every junior in my section of American literature—when I previously had the freedom to let my fifth graders choose books and reading partners—one of my colleagues said, "Why can't you do that with your juniors? A good idea is a good idea, K through 12" (L. Mori, personal communication, 1991). Her words challenged me to stop fretting and do something about it.

However, giving the juniors in my American literature class the choice of books and group members did not go smoothly. When I went to the bookroom to pick up five copies each of half a dozen novels dealing with civil rights, American novelist Toni Morrison's (1987) *Beloved* was not in the stack. Turns out that would have been poaching an honors item. Members of the group who signed up for *Beloved* weren't disappointed; they were furious. They were all young women of color who had requested placement in the honors section and been turned down. The double discrimination ignited the accumulated fuel load of the entire class, and the civil rights movement was hot in the classroom. This might not have been exactly what Dewey (1990) had in mind when he wrote in *The School and Society* that school must become "an embryonic community life, active with types of occupations that reflect the life of the larger society" (p. 29), but it was a start.

Dewey (1900, 1990) and other education reformers of his time wrote that every student in the United States is entitled to a free education. However, the purpose of that education and how best to deliver it remained up in the air, and Americans are still not certain what the promise of a free education for all should look like. But one thing is certain: this promise comes with a cost, primarily to state governments. In order to protect states and localities from insolvency, the national commitment to public education is fulfilled as efficiently as possible. Public education is run like a factory, losing sight of the fact that people—especially young people—can't be assembled from parts along a conveyor belt. The publication of *A Nation at Risk* (National Commission on Excellence in Education, 1983) stimulated a new wave of progressive thinking about how to close down the factory model and rescue students and teachers. Education reform leader Theodore R. Sizer (1984), in the first of the Horace books, *Horace's Compromise*, gives avid readers like myself stunning and inspiring confirmation of our own lives as teachers in a system that prioritizes the institution ahead of those it is intended to serve:

> Horace Smith and his ablest colleagues may be the key to better high schools, but it is respected adolescents who will shape them. Inspiration, hunger: these are the qualities that drive good schools. The best we educational planners can do is to create the most likely conditions for them to flourish, and then get out of their way. (p. 221)

This passage highlights what I have come to believe are two essential qualities of education: (1) respect and (2) agency. For school to be meaningful and for learning to matter, students need teachers in K–12 and across content areas who respect and trust them to make good use of those *likely conditions*. I wish I could report great progress toward the changes needed in policy and practice to shift the emphasis from the institution to the human beings trapped inside the factory model of education, but this model has not collapsed. U.S. students might be at risk, but the inertia of school tradition was and still is surprisingly hard to overcome.

Over time, my experience has convinced me that despite the challenges, taking a student-centered approach is important for all students; they learn better in an environment where teachers respect, know, and support them. So why aren't educators taking a student-centered approach in K–12 and across content areas in every school? Well, because taking a student-centered approach in an effective way isn't easy.

Although the term is often used loosely, a *student-centered approach* does not mean anything goes. To be effective, any approach to teaching must meet challenging criteria, and a student-centered approach is no exception. Not only that, it takes courage and determination to try something new when everyone else seems content to leave things the way they are. But when you keep a steady focus on what you want learning to be like for your students, even your mistakes contribute to your progress. In the early years, I knew something was working when my students' eyes lit up with recognition. They knew their teacher was going out on a limb again to make school meaningful.

Over time I've moved toward criterion-referenced and performance-based assessment because it provides students with shared learning goals and flexible opportunities to demonstrate their growing knowledge and skills. According to the Stanford School Redesign Network (2008):

> Research has shown that such assessment provides useful information about student performance to students, parents, teachers, principals, and policymakers. Research on thinking and learning processes also

shows that performance-based assessment propels the education system in a direction that corresponds with how individuals actually learn.

This type of assessment interweaves naturally with the collaborative spirit of a student-centered classroom. After many years of trial and error, it seems to me there are six interrelated and overlapping practices that work together to create a coherent, effective, and immensely satisfying student-centered approach.

1. **Encourage academic success:** Instead of presenting one-size-fits-all lessons to the entire class, work with individual students and collaborative groups to identify areas of strength and need. Then, you can use this knowledge to help each student experience learning as an integrated, interactive, and individualized process leading to academic success.

2. **Support personal growth:** Instead of directing student learning, serve as a guide and mentor, supporting each student's personal growth as an independent and imaginative thinker and as a unique individual with a strong sense of integrity.

3. **Make space for speaking and listening:** Instead of limiting the curriculum to what standardized tests cover, include opportunities for students to develop speaking and listening skills and the confidence to use them in the larger world.

4. **Deepen understanding with writing and reading:** Instead of using writing to test reading comprehension, help students see writing as a way to deepen understanding of their own lives and make what goes on in the minds of good readers explicit and accessible to students.

5. **Meet individual needs in the evaluation process:** Instead of grading assignments and reporting the average, meet individual student needs with flexible adaptation of tasks and sequence, and provide timely, specific feedback on the work. Work as your students' partner to share evaluation of their progress toward achieving their learning goals.

6. **Communicate with the school community:** Instead of doing things the way they have always been done, look for approaches and strategies that offer students the respect and support they need to fully engage in and enjoy learning. Then, share what you learn with colleagues, administrators, and parents.

These practices form the hub of student-centered teaching, so each chapter of this book focuses on one. At the end of each chapter, you'll find suggestions for next steps—small steps designed to encourage teachers to take ownership of these six student-centered teaching practices. Make them yours!

As you read, you may have questions you can't immediately find an answer for in the text. I have gathered questions teachers ask most often, along with answers, in a handy appendix (page 131). This section gathers the most relevant passages from throughout the book and is designed to be a quick reference that you can check while reading or come back to after you've finished.

Schools and even districts have questioned traditional practices, found alternatives to help students learn, and embraced change. But these are still relatively few. After I retired, I wrote an article that offers information about an alternative to averaged grades (Miller, 2013). The article included my email address, and I still hear from teachers who want to do something similar for their students. This made me realize that schools and districts ready for change might be few, but teachers ready for change are many. I offer this book to those teachers who are looking for practical and philosophical support to take a student-centered approach within a traditional school.

Perhaps the most important thing you'll find in this book is affirmation of your own ideas about what works for students. Although you may be the only person in your building who knows *student centered* doesn't just mean pulling desks into a circle, there are teachers everywhere interested in a student-centered approach. You have company in K–12 schools and across content areas, including teachers of English learners and special education. From the information and anecdotes in this book, you'll find confirmation that you are part of a community of educators who are changing lives in the classroom and creating the potential for a much-needed and long-awaited shift in how teachers approach education. The joy your students find in your student-centered approach will be a game changer for them, and their joy will work wonders for your love of teaching. There is nothing more satisfying than knowing you have created a setting where your students can go deep and reach their full potential.

The student-centered classroom is both a place and a mindset. Whether you and your students gather in a literal room or via video calls, the desire to take a student-centered approach is all you need to begin. Every step you take to share control of their learning with your students will be a step forward. I offer this book to encourage, support, and appreciate the choice you are making to embark on this journey. We'll begin with the first student-centered teaching practice: encourage academic success.

CHAPTER 1

Encourage Academic Success

The practices I discuss in this book are not dangerous or controversial, but they do have the power to change the way your classroom works. There's no need to wait for the system to change. All too often, that wait leads to teacher frustration, exhaustion, and burnout. Students spend most of their time at school in a classroom. You can take that time and make it matter to students. Instead of presenting one-size-fits-all lessons to an entire class, you can work with individual students and collaborative groups to identify areas of strength and need, and help each student experience learning as an integrated, interactive, and individualized process leading to academic success. That's the essence of the first student-centered teaching practice: encourage academic success.

To encourage academic success, a student-centered classroom must provide three key elements: (1) integration of subject matter with student interests, (2) plenty of interaction among students, and (3) individualization to ensure each student feels known and respected. The following sections cover each of these three topics.

Integration With Student Interests

One of the very best reasons for students to come to school each day is the opportunity to interact with peers and adults interested in their experience and ideas. And students who are eager for this kind of interaction provide teachers with a great reason to come to school as well. Taking a student-centered approach invites students' lives into the classroom and uses a variety of resources to provoke, develop, challenge, and deepen ideas. My subject is English, but a student-centered approach can increase student engagement in any content area or grade level.

This approach makes it possible to explore essential ideas in ways relevant and important to students, helping them integrate experiences, concerns, and issues from their own lives with course material. This integration makes learning genuine, unique, and enduring for each student. Students want their work to be meaningful. When assignments are embedded in an engaging, relevant context, students will go as far as they can. For example, my students tended to have difficulty getting into the essays of Ralph Waldo Emerson and Henry David Thoreau, even though their ideas resonate with teenagers. A student-centered approach makes it possible to organize multiple resources on an essential question such as, How do we know what is true? What makes the question *essential* is that it operates on a number of levels. Students can relate to the question and have something to say about it right away. They can keep the question in mind and deepen their response to it as they encounter new material. Finally, and most important, considering the question helps students understand themselves and feel connected to other people, both past and present. My students explored the work of Emerson and Thoreau along with Ray Bradbury's (1953) novel *Fahrenheit 451*, the film *Good Night, and Good Luck* (Heslov & Clooney, 2005), and op-eds and news articles. The range of materials generated many ways for students to connect. Instead of worrying about whether or not each student got every detail, I was able to enjoy spoken and written evidence that each student's unique encounters with important ideas resulted in individual thought and growth.

One way to approach integration of academic topics with individual interests is to anticipate resistance from students that arises from gender expectations, cultural norms, and the habits students have already formed around school. Many years ago, I invited seniors in an honors section of British and world literature to share their opinions about an issue. I don't even remember the issue; what was memorable was who spoke and who didn't. Male students jumped in readily and emphatically; female students declined to participate. The gender line was so marked that I sent the male students for a short walk, so I could speak privately with the female students. Once the big voices left the room, the quiet ones had plenty to say. They complained about aggressive tactics and scoring points instead of striving for understanding. These intelligent, hard-working, ambitious young women had been shouted down so long they simply gave up. They were not, of course, alone. Even though female students tend to earn better grades in elementary and secondary school and outnumber male students in college, they are still underestimated in areas traditionally dominated by men (Cimpian, 2018).

The tendency for different expectations about the performance of female and male students persists even after decades of research and reform. It's still important to make consideration of gender equity a conscious element of planning for the success of all students. Some of the most challenging students I've encountered were boys who saw it as a matter of honor to resist institutional norms. These boys produced thought-provoking essays but didn't follow the directions; they scribbled riddles in their exam books, they recited American poet Allen Ginsberg's (2001) poem "Howl" to the beat of bongo drums, and they copied original poems on bricks and longed to hurl them through windows. Key to the student-centered classroom is trust that every student wants to learn. Creating the most likely conditions for all students to excel requires the teacher's acceptance and appreciation of their individual history and needs.

There's yet another form of resistance to a student-centered approach that requires some teacher diplomacy. Students who've gotten in the habit of taking the path of least resistance may not initially welcome an invitation to think, research, and write about topics of their choice. These students may prefer the status quo of the teacher doing the hard work of generating ideas and designing projects. Author James Moffett (1994) warns that secondary students especially may:

> Resent and resist being asked to do things differently. . . . But if while understanding the reluctance to have the game changed on them midway, you hold a steady course toward their personal responsibility and deep involvement with their own learning, you will see resurrections as gratifying as anything a teacher can experience. (p. 71)

In my work with students, I have seen this proven true over and over again. A student who was so worried about not receiving conventional grades that he requested a meeting with me to argue for them ended up writing eloquently at the end of the year about how much he had learned. Once he realized how much influence he had over what he would learn, he used this freedom well, exploring research and writing about the idea of time and what it means to us as human beings. Although he started out thinking *student centered* was just another word for *more work, less reward*, the integration of his individual interests with course requirements made the work joyful and the reward intrinsic. Another student entered my class so frustrated with academic writing conventions, her first essay was nearly incoherent. First, I convinced her I would not give up on her and, second, that she was trying to write poetry and prose simultaneously. The power and clarity of her work in both genres was astonishing once she was able to separate them. She discovered in herself both a capacity for critical thinking and a genius for original poetry. If you don't let students off the hook by making your own ideas the focus of the class, they are capable of remarkable intersections between what already matters to them and what they are ready and willing to explore. Planning ahead increases the likelihood that students will discover plenty of intersections between their current interests and new ideas and information. The chart in figure 1.1 (page 14) shows how a fifth-grade teacher might anticipate and prevent resistance to a science unit on ecosystems.

Interaction Among Students

A *teacher-directed approach* tends to rely primarily on whole-group instruction the teacher presents or directs. Traditional school classrooms are designed and equipped for this approach. A classroom with thirty desk-chair units arranged in neat rows, all facing the teacher's desk at the front of the room, does not lend itself to a student-centered approach. But the teacher's desk can be in a corner and the rows of desk-chair units

Curriculum goal	Concept of ecosystem and interdependence of plants and animals within a system			
Essential question: What is an ecosystem?	Gender expectations	Cultural norms	Habits of school	Special considerations
Academic text: *The Bacteria Book: The Big World of Really Tiny Microbes* by Steve Mould (2018)	The book makes a scientific topic accessible and engaging.	The author walks the line between interesting and icky. Watch out for stereotypes around the term *ick*.		The book provides scientific background and openings for understanding of the COVID-19 virus.
Contemporary texts: Articles, stories, and poetry related to both positive and negative impacts of humans on ecosystems				Some students may welcome an opening to discuss COVID-19, while others may have experiences that make such discussion traumatic.
Multigenre resources: Films *Hoot* (Marshall, Buffet, & Shriner, 2006) and *WALL-E* (Morris & Stanton, 2008)	Both films have strong female characters.			
Formative activities: Population count of plants and animals within a given area		Consider cultural expectations for dress and conduct outdoors.		
Performance task: A (Modest) Proposal—Research an ecological problem, and propose a solution (satire is an option).			Giving students a summary of *A Modest Proposal* (Swift, 2019) and offering satire as an option may prevent students from treating the project as just another report.	

Figure 1.1: Planning ahead for a fifth-grade science unit.

rotated toward the middle of the room so students face one another. A simple modification like this sends a message: the focus is on students and the interactions between and among them that will challenge and expand their thinking and learning.

For student interaction to become an integral part of classroom structure, students need regular, rich opportunities to confer with other students, creating the conditions where they can share, develop, and express ideas in their work in a more formal way. Although many group configurations are possible (and teachers can spend a lot of time and energy creating groups, rotating group members, and so on), what matters most to students is the opportunity to belong to a long-term collaboration group that provides support and encouragement. It's fine for teachers to allow students to form collaboration groups around existing friendships and affinities. It's also important for students to have regular opportunities to meet with a *peer-conference group*; however, the teacher should determine membership in peer-conference groups based on the strengths and needs of individual students.

To achieve the purposes of both collaborative and peer-conference groups, members must accept responsibility for completing tasks, adhering to group agreed-on due dates, and communicating with other members when there are problems. The teacher's role is to understand the dynamics of each group, not direct its work. As you observe, listen, and visit the groups, look for opportunities to coach students in ways that help them sharpen their skills without reducing their responsibility for the group's success. For example, when one of my students wanted to argue with his peer-conference group that his essay was not missing a thesis because he stated his position in the conclusion, all I needed to do was remind him to simply listen to what the other members offered, make notes, and then decide whether or not revision was warranted. When I noticed a collaboration group mysteriously afflicted with *verbal fillers*—as if they were contagious—I sat in and obnoxiously caught them using *like* or *you know* until they would catch one another and, ultimately, catch and correct themselves. When I heard a student launch an interesting idea in her collaboration group and then cut herself off, saying, "I don't know . . ." I turned to the other members and said, "I think she does know and can explain her idea if you ask her to."

Students hear "Get into your groups" all the time, but in a student-centered classroom where so much of the important work is done in groups, it's better not to assume too much. So student *collaboration* does not to collapse into student *socialization*, it's important to plan ahead for group composition, directions for tasks, and criteria for evaluation. And it's important to specifically include collaboration in the course learning goals. This sends a clear message that how students interact with one another is important, and that progress toward collaboration skills achievement is part of the work each student is responsible for. You can hand out a checklist to your students to help guide them as they engage with their groups. However, students of all ages may benefit from designing their own collaboration learning goals based on prior experience about what works and what doesn't. At the end of each marking period, I asked students to reflect on their learning experience in a State of the Student report. At the end of the first marking period, teachers can ask students to comment on how the collaboration learning goals are working. You might learn, as I did, that students can't meet some of the goals because they're too vague or there just aren't opportunities to address them in the classroom. If this is the case, it's time to turn the task over to the students and let them revise the goals.

Figure 1.2 provides an example of collaboration learning goals for elementary students. Figure 1.3 shows some possible collaboration learning goals for secondary students.

Put a check mark next to each item that describes you as a group member. It's OK to leave some items blank. The purpose of the checklist is to celebrate your strengths and figure out what you need to work on.

☐ I treat each group member with respect.

☐ I listen to what other group members say.

☐ I am honest and kind when I speak.

☐ I am ready to lead and to follow.

☐ When I make a promise, I keep it.

Figure 1.2: Collaboration learning goals for elementary students example.

*Visit **go.SolutionTree.com/instruction** for a free reproducible version of this figure.*

Students must appreciate the impact their group work participation can have on the quality of their own long-term education, as well as the quality of fellow group members' day-to-day experience. The teacher should actively monitor student groups, to both troubleshoot and comment when students do their jobs well. In the larger world of college and careers, having the ability to interact effectively with others that results from well organized, sustained group work is highly portable and has the potential to open doors.

Although there are many terms for *group work—collaboration, cooperation, discussion, peer conference, project-based learning, text-based seminar*, and so on—what matters is the contribution each group configuration makes to student learning. In my experience, two group configurations make the most significant contributions to learning: (1) the collaboration group, which tackles daily activities and group projects; and (2) the peer-conference group, which provides feedback on work in progress. Both configurations create conditions where students can learn from one another.

You will probably meet some of these goals through the natural give-and-take of collaboration. But some goals will require conscious thought and effort. In the Comments column, leave a note to yourself about each goal. How are you doing? What have you tried? What would you do differently next time? Give yourself credit for what you're doing well, and look for things you'd like to do better.

Collaboration learning goals	Comments
Act responsibly with the interests of the larger community in mind.	
Deal positively with praise, setbacks, and criticism.	
Demonstrate the ability to work effectively with diverse teams.	
Be open and responsive to new and diverse perspectives; incorporate group input and feedback.	
Exercise flexibility and willingness to be helpful in making necessary compromises to accomplish a common goal.	
Set and meet high standards and goals for delivering quality work on time.	
Assume shared responsibility for collaborative work.	
Adapt to varied roles and responsibilities.	

Source: Adapted from Partnership for 21st Century Learning, 2019.

Figure 1.3: Collaboration learning goals for secondary students example.

Visit **go.SolutionTree.com/instruction** *for a free reproducible version of this figure.*

Collaboration Group

Working together to get things done might seem like a natural aspect of being human, something we can take for granted. But really effective collaboration requires conscious effort and willingness to share success as well as support. In *Limitless Mind*, Jo Boaler (2019b) shares two anecdotes that underscore both the importance of collaboration and the need to teach it as an essential skill. First, she recounts how when he was on the mathematics faculty at University of California, Berkeley, Uri Treisman noticed that 60 percent of African American students who took calculus were failing, which sometimes led to students dropping out of college altogether. He also noticed that the failure rate for Chinese Americans was zero. When he asked colleagues why there should be such a discrepancy, they came up with predictable socio-economic differences between the two cultures. But when Treisman studied how students worked on mathematics problems, he discovered that Chinese American students worked together, while African American students worked alone. Treisman and his team set up workshops to help students learn to work collaboratively. Within two years, the failure rate dropped from 60 percent to zero. Collaboration provides support and the opportunity to build on shared knowledge and skills. Second, a large-scale international test of mathematical ability in fifteen-year-olds appeared to show that girls scored much lower than boys. When anxiety was factored in, the gap in scores disappeared. And when students were tested on collaboration problem solving, building on ideas with a computer agent, girls flourished. Boaler (2019a) comments, "This research reveals the potential of collaboration, not only for girls or students of color, but for all learners and thinkers. When you connect with someone else's ideas, you enhance your brain, your understanding, and your perspective."

Although it's been around for a while, the detailed discussion of group work in *Student-Centered Language Arts, K–12* (Moffett & Wagner, 1992) is especially useful; I followed the recommendation of five students for most small-group work: "For most discussions, around five is an ideal number, providing enough variety of viewpoint to stimulate interaction but at the same time minimizing the risk of shy individuals retiring because the group is too large" (p. 51). A group of three can work, although the conversation may not be as varied or rich as it would be with more members. Groups of four can also work as long as they don't divide into groups of two. It's important to respect each student's individual style, from outgoing to reserved, but active participation in a small group is a low-risk activity that can build student confidence and skill, which will then transfer to higher-risk performances and presentations.

When students compose their own collaboration groups you can encourage them to look for varied strengths and weaknesses in their potential collaboration group members, as well as personal affinity and trust, but I left the decision about group membership up to students. If personal affinity develops into a romantic interest, you need to pay even closer attention to group dynamics. I encouraged students involved in a relationship not to join the same collaboration group, but both parties always talked me out of it. In most cases, the work went on even after the relationship ended. In one case, another collaboration group adopted one student after a breakup. Because the purpose of this group is to provide consistent support and growing understanding of individual potential and goals over the course of the year, it's generally not a problem for close friends to work together, as they take a serious interest in one another's progress. Occasionally, group members may reinforce one another's weaknesses rather than bolster one another's strengths. If that happens, it's time for honest discussion and, when necessary, reconfiguration. The teacher can address situations like these without wresting control from group members. When members have completed a project together, ask them to reflect. See figure 1.4 for a reflection tool that students can use to record their thinking.

How did you decide on the role each group member would play?	
Did group members meet your expectations for creativity and responsibility?	
Did you encounter any problems with the process your group used to plan and carry out the project?	
Did the final product meet your expectations?	
How could you improve the guidelines, process, or presentation of this project?	

Figure 1.4: Collaboration group reflection questions.

*Visit **go.SolutionTree.com/instruction** for a free reproducible version of this figure.*

Peer-Conference Group

When I attended the University of California, Berkeley's Bay Area Writing Project Summer Open Program in the 1980s, the idea of writing as a process rather than a one-shot deal was still new. Part of this process is giving the writer opportunities to get feedback while a piece is still in draft form. This feedback can come from both the teacher and a group of peers. When the summer program concluded, I had a thick folder of handouts that continued to grow over the intervening decades. Along with recognizing that writing is a process, educators realize this process is useful across content areas, whether it's explaining the thinking that went into solving a mathematics problem, analyzing the results of a science lab, or imagining letters a teenage girl working in a New England textile mill might have written to an older brother in California panning for gold in the 1850s.

Regardless of subject area, it's important for students to read their work in progress aloud. Because their pieces tend to be shorter and simpler, elementary students can read an entire draft while secondary students might need to circulate a printed copy ahead of time and limit the reading aloud to a key section, perhaps one giving the writer difficulty. The most powerful form of feedback I've encountered is also spoken. After hearing a piece, listeners say back to the writer what they heard. This simple, direct process can tell the writer whether or not the intended information, message, or attitude is coming across to readers. Students usually find the process of giving and getting responses on work in progress both natural and engaging, so they don't need lots of steps or directions. The guidelines I used for peer-conference groups were whittled down over the years to serve just as reminders of what students might ask or offer. It's worth noting the peer-conference group is important not just for the feedback each student receives but also for the exposure to others' ideas, organizational strategies, style, use of humor, and so on. The work in progress under consideration need not always be a piece of writing. It could be a plan for a science experiment, a survey of student preferences regarding after-school programs, a diagram of a mathematics problem, an idea for a drawing, the lyrics for a song, or an infinite number of other possibilities. In figure 1.5 and figure 1.6, you will find the guidelines I developed for both elementary and secondary students. The guidelines for secondary students (see figure 1.6) are not much different from those for elementary students (see figure 1.5) except for addressing paper management related to the secondary students' potential for longer drafts.

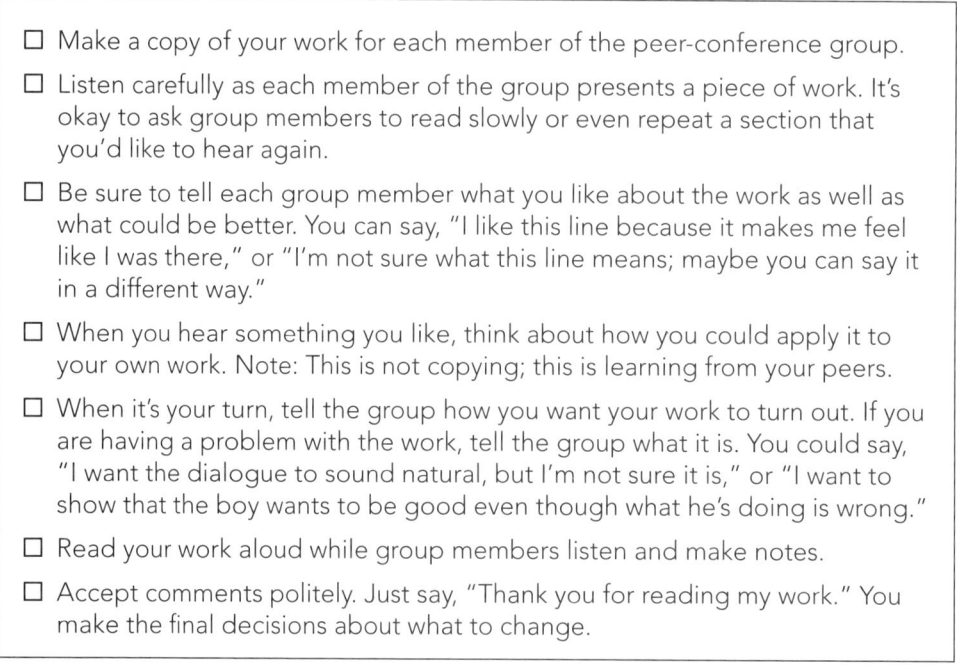

- ☐ Make a copy of your work for each member of the peer-conference group.
- ☐ Listen carefully as each member of the group presents a piece of work. It's okay to ask group members to read slowly or even repeat a section that you'd like to hear again.
- ☐ Be sure to tell each group member what you like about the work as well as what could be better. You can say, "I like this line because it makes me feel like I was there," or "I'm not sure what this line means; maybe you can say it in a different way."
- ☐ When you hear something you like, think about how you could apply it to your own work. Note: This is not copying; this is learning from your peers.
- ☐ When it's your turn, tell the group how you want your work to turn out. If you are having a problem with the work, tell the group what it is. You could say, "I want the dialogue to sound natural, but I'm not sure it is," or "I want to show that the boy wants to be good even though what he's doing is wrong."
- ☐ Read your work aloud while group members listen and make notes.
- ☐ Accept comments politely. Just say, "Thank you for reading my work." You make the final decisions about what to change.

Figure 1.5: Peer-conference group guidelines for elementary students.

*Visit **go.SolutionTree.com/instruction** for a free reproducible version of this figure.*

Guidelines for presenters	Guidelines for group members
Before the peer conference	
☐ Prepare a draft of the work in progress for the group to consider. ☐ Distribute copies of longer pieces to readers ahead of time in class or via email or social media.	☐ If you receive a copy of the draft ahead of time, set aside time to look it over and make written notes. ☐ Highlight what you like about the content and style as well as areas that might need attention.
During the peer conference	
☐ Briefly explain what you're trying to accomplish with the piece, and mention questions or concerns about it. Read the entire piece aloud or a section of the piece that is not working well. ☐ Listen and take written notes on the group members' comments about the piece. ☐ Ask group members follow-up questions. ☐ Ask group members to return their marked-up copies of the piece to you, so you can refer to them during revision.	☐ Make written notes of concerns or questions the presenter raises. ☐ Listen carefully when the presenter reads the draft or a section aloud. Tell the presenter what you heard. ☐ Draw on your written notes to discuss the strengths and needs of the piece with the presenter and other group members.
After the peer conference	
☐ Review the group members' comments and written notes. You don't have to use every suggestion. Decide what will help you make the work in progress better.	☐ Look for opportunities to apply what you learned from others to your own work.

Figure 1.6: Peer-conference guidelines for secondary students.

*Visit **go.SolutionTree.com/instruction** for a free reproducible version of this figure.*

Staging a demonstration of a bad peer conference is a way to underscore the level of attention students need to make a peer conference worthwhile to all participants. Ask five students to follow the directions in figure 1.7 (page 22), which require students to engage in hilarious violations of the peer-conference guidelines. Then, invite the rest of the class to debrief what was bad about the peer-conference demonstration and what needs to change for a peer conference to go well.

Script for Presenter
Say things like, "I don't know what you should look for . . . whatever . . . it's not very good anyway . . . I scribbled it in half an hour the night before it was due."

In response to group member three, get defensive. Say something like, "I can't believe you said that. You've got to be kidding. I mean that's so hurtful. Maybe my idea is a little unclear, but you didn't have to say so!"

Script for Group Member One
Raise your hand to give feedback first. Say something like, "It was really great . . . I wouldn't change a thing." Then hold the draft in front of your face to conceal the fact that you are taking a quick nap and gradually fall asleep with the draft as your head pillow.

Script for Group Member Two
Use the draft to partially conceal the fact that you are working on another assignment. Ask group member three for help on this assignment. When it's your turn to provide feedback, say something like, "It's really good, just add a little more detail," and then go back to the homework.

Script for Group Member Three
Say something like, "Look, I have to be honest . . . that's the point of peer conference . . . your piece is pretty random. I read it four times and still don't know what it's about."

Script for Group Member Four
For the entire time, turn your back to the peer-conference group, and chat with someone nearby who is not in the group. When it's your turn to speak, say something like, "Everybody already said what I was going to say."

Figure 1.7: Directions for demonstrating a bad peer conference.

*Visit **go.SolutionTree.com/instruction** for a free reproducible version of this figure.*

Some educated guesswork will help you set up the first round of peer-conference groups. At the beginning of the year, I asked my students to complete a survey designed to get a sense of their attitudes toward English class. I wanted students to write candid responses to the survey questions rather than try to figure out the "right" answer or what I wanted to see, so I made the questions broad and asked for just a couple of sentences in response. See figure 1.8 for a template with examples of survey questions students could receive. These questions could easily be modified to fit any subject or grade level.

How do you describe yourself as a reader?	
How do you describe yourself as a writer?	
How do you describe yourself as a speaker and performer?	
How do you describe yourself as a listener?	
How to you describe yourself as a researcher?	
How do you describe yourself as a participant in a group project?	
What is the most important thing you learned in your English class last year?	
What would you like to learn in English class this year?	
If you could change one thing about English class, what would it be?	

Figure 1.8: Attitude survey for an English class.

*Visit **go.SolutionTree.com/instruction** for a free reproducible version of this figure.*

By noting how positive or negative students were in their replies, I avoided creating groups that concentrated students with negative comments. The peer-conference groups should be about the same size as collaboration groups so everyone will get about ten minutes of feedback in a fifty-minute workshop. As you learn more about each student, forming groups that include members with different strengths and weaknesses gets easier. One problem I ran into was the sense of isolation that some more proficient students felt. They gave a great deal to their groups, but the feedback they were getting was not challenging them to go beyond what they were already so good at. As the whole class develops stronger skills, you can take less care with balancing the composition of peer-conference groups so each one includes students with needs and students with strengths. When the class reaches this point, it's possible to invite students with an exceptional affinity for the subject to work together without depriving the other groups of strong role models.

The combination of collaboration and peer-conference groups provides each student with support and suggestions and offers each class member the opportunity to contribute substantially to the quality of the learning his or her classmates experience.

Individualization to Ensure Students Feel Known and Respected

In a traditional classroom, the teacher makes decisions about lessons, assignments, tests, and grades. The teacher's personal areas of interest and experience will likely influence unit designs. Students often respond positively to the teacher's enthusiasm. What more can we ask? Researchers and authors Grant Wiggins and Jay McTighe's (2005) model of lesson design outlined in *Understanding by Design* helps teachers realize that these "pet units" might be fun, but they don't necessarily result in the enduring understanding of key concepts and skills that students need. Once you've asked yourself what a class needs to develop enduring understanding, you don't have to go much farther to wonder what each student might need. And the best way to find out is to *ask the student*. The result can be a powerful partnership between teacher and student that makes it possible to achieve important learning goals in both efficient and enjoyable ways.

"But," teachers may argue, "it takes a lot of time to get to know students well enough to individualize their work, and I'm already working long hours, seven days a week." So where can you find more time? Ask yourself what you're spending time on that you could give up because not doing it won't have a negative impact on students. I'd be willing to bet you'll come up with the same answer I did—and that answer will make you feel a little shaky at first. I'll bet you spend the most time on what has the least impact on student learning: grading. When I finally worked up the courage to stop grading every single assignment, I had time to confer with students, understand their strengths and needs, and individualize tasks and projects. I also had time for more detailed written comments about work in progress. In chapter 5 (page 89), you'll find a detailed discussion of why it's not only OK but also really important to provide detailed feedback instead of grades.

Now that you've gotten some grounding in using integration, interaction, and individualization to encourage academic success in the classroom, we can move on in the next chapter to the second of six student-centered teaching practices: support personal growth.

Next Steps for Encouraging Academic Success

If you attend to three elements—integration, interaction, and individualization—you can create a classroom environment all students deserve. The following tool details some steps you can take to experiment with integration, interaction, and individualization in your classroom. For each step, note the date you tried it and reflect on how it went: What did you do? How did it go? What would you change? What's next? There are spaces available at the end for you to plan additional steps you can take toward a student-centered approach to teaching.

Next Steps Tried	Date Tried	Reflection
Survey students about their learning styles, personal interests, and what they hope to learn in your class.		
Organize a unit of study about a question that taps into students' interests.		
Try collaborative groups for one marking period. Let students know you will be monitoring the groups and the quality of their group work will determine whether they continue to work in groups.		
Let students know you will not be grading one type of assignment—for example, lab notes, journal entries, or mathematics facts—but you will make comments and save their work.		

The Student-Centered Classroom © 2021 Solution Tree Press • SolutionTree.com
Visit **go.SolutionTree.com/instruction** to download this free reproducible.

CHAPTER 2

Support Personal Growth

In his last book, *The Universal Schoolhouse*, Moffett (1994) laments the lack of forward movement in public schools as "a discouraging twenty-five years trying to reform just their teaching of literacy and language" (p. 59). All the same, Moffett's (1994) vision of public education continues to expand, and schools must remain at the center of that vision:

> Public education reaches everybody and for a long time during the formative years. What it does or does not do is extremely important. Its influence is second only to the home, and in the most important cases—where home hardly exists—some schools already provide a safer, warmer, and more stable environment, the prerequisite for learning. These havens point the way to broader, curative education. (pp. 59–60)

I heard Moffett speak at a conference in 1991 and pounced on a copy of the fourth edition of *Student-Centered Language Arts, K–12*, the big why-to and how-to book he wrote with Betty Jane Wagner (1992). What I learned from their passionate ideas and practical suggestions helped me get serious about taking a student-centered approach. Gradually, I realized that within an institution designed for efficiency, there could be places designed for humanity, places where students would know one another and their teachers well, places where students would feel safe to take risks, to think and write, and to speak and listen about issues of real concern. In such a classroom, students would be free to flex their growing capacity for independent thought, exercise their imaginations, and develop the personal integrity that ultimately provides ethical grounding for society as a whole. These havens could have an immediate, beneficial impact on the students and, over time, might become the source of bottom-up reform. As public school advocates Emily Gasoi and Deborah Meier (2018) remind us:

> Ultimately, the purpose of public education in a democracy is to get more Americans, starting in early childhood, to internalize the idea that they are part of the deciding class, as entitled as anyone else to voice an opinion and to make a mark on the world. That, of course, is the ideal—one worth striving for.

These considerations make up the second student-centered teaching practice: support personal growth. *Personal growth* requires making the classroom a safe place for students to explore and develop qualities that make us human and keep us whole. Instead of directing student learning, the teacher serves as a guide and mentor, supporting each student's growth as a unique individual and nurturing his or her developing independence, imagination, and integrity. The following sections cover each of these three topics in turn.

Independent Thinking

It's a natural element of a student-centered teaching approach to offer students a voice in project design and choices in their topics. In a student-centered classroom, the teacher chooses to share authority with students and to expect at least glimpses of students' full potential. In an article about strategies teachers can use to teach independent thinking, Margaret Regan (2013), teacher and founder of Martha's Vineyard Master Teaching Institute, focuses on a study of people who find satisfaction with their lives conducted by psychologist Mihaly Csikszentmihalyi. He defines those who are happiest when they are absorbed in complex activities as *autotelic*. Regan (2013) points out:

> The most significant factor for autotelic development is what Csikszentmihalyi terms *attentional capacity*. Consequently, if his research into self-motivated learning is correct, then the classroom should become an incubator for growing students' attentional capacity. . . . By testing and analyzing unique ideas, the classroom can grow students' attentional capacity and show them the value of and methods for thinking independently. . . . This is what we must do if we want schools to fulfill their purpose: developing young minds that have been assured new ideas are exciting and worth pursuing.

To convince your students you truly welcome independent thought, you must provide opportunities for them to think and write in ways that lesson plans do not predetermine. Teachers should let go of some of their authority as the subject-area expert. The work you ask students to engage in can't confine them to the content and skills you already know well. When students have genuine opportunities to voice their opinions and make choices, the potential for their perceptions and insights to take you by surprise increases. It feels a little awkward to respond to a student's idea by admitting, "I never thought of that," or "That's not the way I see it," instead of saying, "That's incorrect," but it's thrilling to see students think for themselves. Of course, teenagers are capable of wild ideas that do need a different kind of feedback, but they are also capable of broadening their teachers' horizons as well as their own. I was recently in contact with a student who was in a section of American literature that I taught early in my career. One of the books we read as a class was Tim O'Brien's (1990)

The Things They Carried. As a war story, I thought the book would be especially engaging to male readers, and I knew there were some reluctant readers among the male students in the class. What I learned from my former student was that he loved O'Brien's book, not because it was about war, but because it was about being an adult in a complex, often ambiguous world (M. Henss, personal communication, April 27, 2020).

It's not easy to give students the kind of space—literal and metaphoric—they need to develop as independent thinkers. There are times when the idea of rows of dutiful, obedient students working away at their desks without making a peep sounds just wonderful. There are many benefits to gathering students in rooms with knowledgeable, caring adults, but managing the pragmatic needs of large numbers can be challenging. Typical approaches to crowd control tend to provoke instinctive, unreasoned resistance (that is, *us or them*). A student-centered approach always seeks *all of us*. Recognizing what students may have been dealing with before they enter your student-centered classroom will help you find the courage and patience to continue. Before long, students will come to view your classroom as a haven, a place where there's nothing to resist except the habit of resistance.

To foster independent thought, I make a point of calling the information I give students about assignments *guidelines* rather than *directions*. Figure 2.1, for example, shows a long list of steps students could take to develop an essay.

☐ Brainstorm possible topics.
☐ Select three topics that you care and are curious about.
☐ Ask group members which topic they think would be the most interesting to work on.
☐ Write down everything you already know about the chosen topic.
☐ Read what you wrote to group members, and ask them for questions about your topic.
☐ Consult reliable sources to find answers to your group members' questions.
☐ Record the author, title, publisher, and date of sources. Include page numbers of paginated sources.
☐ Take notes, being careful to place direct quotations in quotation marks.
☐ Write what you have learned about your topic.
☐ Support what you have written with references to sources.
☐ Support what you have written with direct quotations from sources.
☐ Compile a list of sources used in your writing.

Figure 2.1: Guidelines for an essay assignment.

*Visit **go.SolutionTree.com/instruction** for a free reproducible version of this figure.*

You could insist students provide evidence they have completed every step, or you could let students select the steps helpful to them as individuals, with different ways of generating ideas and different approaches to research and writing. Even if you don't feel comfortable inviting students to pick and choose from your list, you can accept deviations when students produce the results you have in mind. It's tempting to feel peeved when students diverge from guidelines you worked hard to develop, but it's important to send the clear message: you want students to be free to think about how to tackle the assignment, rather than just checking boxes.

Independence in the animal world means being able to fend for yourself in very basic terms of food and shelter and, with any luck, finding a mate and some territory that isn't already occupied. Going off on your own is a given. Animals learn how to do this from observation, instruction, and instinct. In the human world, independence is not a given. We have to want independence and earn it on multiple levels— emotional, economic, intellectual. This is a process that begins as we learn to reflect on our own actions, temper independence with compassion, and, eventually, become the wise elders on whom others can rely for seasoned perspectives and sound advice (Korkki, 2014). The definition of wisdom that was developed by Vivian Clayton when she was a neuropsychology graduate student in the 1970s continues to serve as the foundation of research in this field. Based on her own research with ancient texts and recognized decision makers such as lawyers and judges, Clayton defined wisdom as the combination of cognition, reflection, and compassion (Korkki, 2014). Like other aspects of maturing, there are no guarantees. It's possible to be old and foolish, just as it's possible to be wise beyond one's years. Laura L. Carstensen, psychology professor and founding director of the Stanford Center on Longevity, says that if you are wise, "you're not only regulating your emotional state, you're also attending to another person's emotional state" (as cited in Korkki, 2014). She adds, "You're not focusing so much on what you need and deserve, but on what you can contribute" (as cited in Korkki, 2014).

Secondary students are deep in the process of coming to grips with the idea that human beings can simultaneously be autonomous and interdependent. The struggle to find equilibrium between the two can be painful for teenagers and the relationships with family and friends that they simultaneously want to embrace and leave behind. Yet as part of this process, students are developing the capacity to care not only about their own needs but about how they can contribute to the greater good. In an article for *Educational Leadership*, "Assessing What Matters," psychologist and psychometrician Robert J. Sternberg (2008) argues, "Wisdom is the most important and yet most neglected aspect of education today" (p. 25). Sternberg (2008) explains there's nothing wrong with the traditional focus on analytical skills, but teachers shouldn't stop there. For example, a science teacher might ask students to analyze evidence of climate change and then call on students to come up with ways to address climate change in their daily lives. The former requires close examination of the facts while the latter requires independent thought. Sternberg (n.d.) concludes a summary of his work on wisdom called "Balance Theory of Wisdom," by asserting that though many see analytical intelligence as most important, wisdom may be even more valuable. He states:

> When citizens and leaders fail in the pursuit of their duties, it is more likely to be for lack of wisdom than for lack of analytical intelligence. . . . In other words, they fail not for a lack of conventional intelligence, but rather for a lack of wisdom. (Sternberg, n.d.)

If Sternberg's observation is correct, wisdom should be at the top of the list of 21st century skills. The findings of researchers such as Csikszentmihalyi, Clayton, Carstensen, and Sternberg (n.d., 2008) demonstrate that educators can assess wisdom, and the information from such assessments is a more accurate predictor of student success in college than conventional measures such as the Scholastic Assessment Test (SAT). Sternberg's (2008) research suggests students are ready to engage deeply across content areas on the issues and ideas of the day. Teachers just have to ask! However, this shift from a teacher-directed to a student-centered approach can be especially challenging for teachers. It takes a double helping of humility to accept responsibility as the adult in charge, and yet remain open to the possibility that the oldest person in the room might not always be the wisest. Sometimes, but not always. Even elementary students have the capacity to come up with a solution to a problem that never occurred to an older person. Encouraging independent thought in students helps them develop wisdom and sends an important message: we want our students to be successful in school because we hope what they learn will help them become the individuals they want to be.

Imaginative Freedom

As editor of *English Journal*, Ken Lindblom poses a particularly interesting question to readers and contributors in the November 2009 issue: Have we killed imagination? Imagination is right up there with creativity, originality, innovation, and invention. These are all qualities that generate a certain awe, qualities great artists and technological entrepreneurs possess, qualities we often think you must be born with because they can't be taught. As someone who has never been able to sing on key, I would have to agree there are some things some people just aren't going to get good at. But I don't believe that should stop teachers, especially teachers who have chosen a student-centered setting, from providing opportunities for students to find out how it feels to take an imaginative leap.

In *The Myth of the Muse*, coauthors Douglas Reeves and Brooks Reeves (2017) take issue with the idea that creativity is innate—you either have it or you don't. They dismantle the widely held misconception that logical and creative functions are assigned to separate hemispheres in our brains and that only individuals whose right brain is dominant are creative. The workings of the brain are much more elaborate than that:

> While it is true that some control of speech is localized in the right hemisphere, the brain is a much more complicated machine than the hemispheric theory suggests. The left and right portions of our brains don't operate in isolation, but instead work together to form our thoughts and ideas. (Reeves & Reeves, 2017, p. 15)

Rather than a flash of inspiration, the Reeves team defines creativity as a "process of experimentation, evaluation, and follow-through that leads to a significant discovery, insight, or contribution" (Reeves & Reeves, 2017, p. 17), and this process, they argue, is one in which everyone can engage. It's not only something that great thinkers throughout history have used to contribute to society; it's a way for all people to connect with themselves and with their communities (Reeves & Reeves, 2017).

The truth is that teachers aren't sure imagination should be welcome in school. And neither are students. Compliance takes a lot less time and energy than a cognitive leap, and a five-paragraph essay is a lot easier to write than a passionate argument. Imagination can be unruly and, worst of all, difficult to assess. The move toward rubrics for assignments grew, at least in part, out of a genuine desire to help students succeed in school by sharing information with them. But it's hard to write a rubric that doesn't descend into meaningless increments of *few*, *some*, and *many*, and a good rubric takes hours of committee work. If teachers acknowledge imagination as something they value in school, will they have to assign and assess it? I think we should be wary of the monster we might create in writing rubrics that make the importance of imagination explicit; we owe it to our students to find a better way than adding an *Imagination* row to a rubric. For imagination to be welcome in the classroom, teachers need to convince students they have the time and energy to engage imaginatively in schoolwork. My experience suggests this will not happen unless there is some convincing give-and-take on the part of teachers about the nature of that work. As Reeves and Reeves (2017) put it:

> Schools rarely undermine creativity intentionally. After all, vision and mission statements extolling the virtues of creativity are ubiquitous. But when we compared the good intentions of schools as they aspired to enhance creativity with their actual behavior (Reeves, 2015), we found an enormous gap between rhetoric and reality. (p. 2)

In order to convince students you mean it when you say you're open to them using their imaginations, try giving them some latitude with their assignments. Let students know what you're looking for and how the assignment contributes to their progress toward achieving learning goals, but then let them come up with the details. Reeves and Reeves (2017) agree: "Because students are often more interested in one subject than another, it makes sense to try to use their individual aptitudes across the spectrum" (p. 52).

Let's say you're a social studies teacher and you want your ninth graders to grapple with the idea that history is subject to interpretation, both by those who were present and shared their perceptions of what happened and by those who came later and realize the accounts vary or even conflict with one another. You could assign a single important event, give students a list of events to choose from, or invite students to brainstorm moments in history they'd like to know more about and, with some guidance from you, pick their topic. The form their findings take could range from a traditional report to a mock newspaper to a play in which they reenact events. You can suggest possibilities and be open to additional ideas from students. The point is that if your goal is understanding of an essential concept rather than memorization of dates and names, students can get where you want them to go by more than one route. Reeves and Reeves (2017) point out that giving students some control over the design of their work is highly motivating. And even if you're not comfortable inviting students to take a divergent path, you can still refrain from penalizing them for doing so if the other path gets them where they need to go.

Collaboration is central to a student-centered classroom, especially when you're hoping to give students opportunities to exercise their imaginations. We have collective images in our minds of what creativity looks like, such as "the rogue painter slaving away in her studio, brandishing a brush, and the gaunt writer hunched like a gargoyle over his laptop" (Reeves & Reeves, 2017, p. 67), but the creative history of humankind has a vast number of examples of collaborative creation as well. Working in a collaborative group gives students access to the power inherent in broaching an idea, listening to what others have to say, and building on one another's experience and suggestions to create something that might not have been possible for a student working alone. Reeves and Reeves (2017) even suggest that the common good depends on creative minds working together to solve the multitude of problems the world faces.

While there are many amazing works of fiction in which writers have imagined entire worlds, leaps of imagination are also responsible for many things we've learned to take for granted in the world we actually inhabit: antibiotics, the telephone, and batteries, for example. These inventions occurred because people wondered about things, grappled with possibilities, and came up with something new. A simple exercise can help students exercise their imaginations as they tap into the evidence of imagination that is all around them. Ask students to close their eyes and imagine that all the objects in the classroom are gone and only the people remain. Are the people floating in midair? When the chairs go away, do people plop to the floor? Do people sit, stand, swim through the air? Then invite students to bring the objects that were in the room back, one by one. Where did the pencil sharpener come from? Who came up with the idea of connecting a desk with a chair? What sequence of thought resulted in motion sensors that turn lights on and off? And so on.

The ability to look beyond *what is* to *what might be* is one of the distinguishing characteristics of humankind. There are classic examples, such as Leonardo da Vinci imagining people could fly and drawing studies of the wing structures of birds to figure out how this could happen. And there are examples close to home, such as an elementary school student imagining what it's like to be a butterfly emerging from its chrysalis and pumping up its wings. Encourage students to ask, "What if? What if butterflies could talk? What if people bounced like balls? What if a clock could soften and droop over the edge of a table? What if a person could wear a computer on her wrist? What if there was a smart vaccine that protected us from everything?" Lindblom's (2009) question, Have we killed imagination?, suggests that encouraging independent thought might not be enough. It might also be important to welcome evidence of imagination in students' work. Writing and sharing what we imagine carries a high degree of risk, yet sharing exactly what makes us each most unique can be immensely moving and satisfying. As students become accustomed to working in a student-centered environment, they learn to count on their peers and teacher to listen intently, respond respectfully, and celebrate their courage as well as their imaginative leaps.

Integrity

It would be hard to find anyone—student, parent, teacher, administrator, or community member—who would not agree that teachers want students to grow up to be good and do good. Yet, there is little agreement about the role teachers should play in helping students understand the importance of integrity. Certainly, students must honestly acknowledge the infinitude of sources they can access with contemporary technology. Students need to use these sources to guide and support their thinking rather than replacing their own processes with the works of others. Yet there is so much more to integrity than honest technology use.

Human beings learn how to make good decisions in much the same way we acquire language—through imitation, experimentation, and instruction. Both elementary and secondary students can benefit from low-risk opportunities to practice making decisions. Andrew Quist and decision scientist Robin Gregory (2019) argue, "Decision making itself needs to be viewed as a skill, one that can be learned through a sequence of guided steps much as driving a car or speaking a new language can be learned" and that schools need to play an active role in teaching this essential skill. Gregory's team identifies three characteristics that are fundamental to effective decision making: (1) a focus on values, (2) awareness that facts need to be accurate, and (3) a mindset open to alternatives (Quist & Gregory, 2019). In collaboration with the Delta School District in British Columbia, Gregory and his colleagues have worked with students in grades 1 through 12 to introduce six steps to the practice of thoughtful decision making (Quist & Gregory, 2019).

1. **Framing:** What is the problem, and how can we frame it as a choice?
2. **Objectives:** What things do we care about could this decision affect?
3. **Alternatives:** What alternatives can we consider?
4. **Consequences:** What are the likely consequences of different courses of action?
5. **Preferences:** How do we feel about the trade-offs? What do we like best, all things considered?
6. **Adapting:** What could trigger us to reconsider, reassess, or adapt our behaviors?

Figure 2.2 contains a tool you can use to introduce these steps to students in your classroom.

As you work through the steps on your own and with your group, keep in mind what is valuable to you, check your facts, and remember to bring an open mind to discussion and decision making.	
Step	**Your notes**
Framing	
Objectives	
Alternatives	
Consequences	
Preferences	
Adapting	

Source: Quist & Gregory, 2019.

Figure 2.2: Six steps to the practice of thoughtful decision making.

*Visit **go.SolutionTree.com/instruction** for a free reproducible version of this figure.*

According to University of California, Berkeley, psychology professor Alison Gopnik, secondary students, especially, need opportunities to practice making decisions in order to find a balance between their emotions and motivations and their ability to exercise self-control (Levinson, 2012). As secondary students develop into adults, what motivates them evolves. As teenagers, their primary motivation is their desire for the respect of their peers. As adults, they will need the self-control to think through emotions and make independent decisions. In order to make this transition, Gopnik (2012) writes in the *Wall Street Journal*: "You come to make better decisions by making not-so-good decisions and then correcting them. You get to be a good planner by making plans, implementing them and seeing the results again and again. Expertise comes with experience."

It's difficult to discuss what it means to be a good person without some discussion of personal beliefs. For secondary students who are grappling with developing an identity that allows them to remain part of a family and simultaneously achieve independence as an individual, support for addressing such important issues in discussion and in writing helps give them and their school experience a sense of wholeness. In my subject area, the poetry of Emily Dickinson is a useful case in point. It's possible to cherry-pick poems that comment on everyday life or the natural world, but any honest look at Dickinson's work must include her personal beliefs. Every biography of more than a few paragraphs includes the fact that she experienced doubts about organized religion fairly early in her life (Emily Dickinson Museum, n.d.). To gloss over such matters is to waste an opportunity for students to connect with a unique American poet and feel the enduring resonance of the questions that troubled her. If students can connect with the inner world of a figure like Emily Dickinson, it can help them understand their own inner worlds. In a student-centered setting, mutual trust and respect provide some latitude for students to invite not just the outer world but also their inner worlds into the classroom.

A specific ethical challenge too many students are likely to experience is how to respond to bullying, whether it happens in a school hallway or restroom or arrives over the internet in the form of social media posts. One of the many benefits of shifting from a teacher-directed to a student-centered approach is the opportunity it provides for students to spend significant time working in collaborative groups. In my own experience, even students who are already friends get to know one another from a new perspective when they work together over the course of a year. And the opportunity for the teacher to get to know students as individuals is heightened by moving away from the front of the room to observe and drop in for visits with collaborative groups. Members of a student's collaboration group might be the first to hear of a troubling incident, and they might serve as the first line of defense against the fear and self-doubt bullies often provoke in victims. Making sure each student belongs to an encouraging, supportive group means no student is alone when problems arise. It may also increase the likelihood that students will seek adult help when those problems are as serious as bullying. I found that students rarely came to me for advice without having first shared concerns with group members who, in turn, encouraged and supported sharing their troubling situations with me. In an atmosphere of trust and respect, students can tackle the related problem of what to do when they are not the victim but the witness of bullying. Like so many ethical questions, there is no rote right answer, but students who've had the opportunity to think, speak, write, and listen to one another on such issues are better prepared to do what makes sense when such a difficult and potentially dangerous situation arises.

Making the shift from a traditional to a student-centered classroom doesn't happen overnight, but each step has its rewards. As your focus as a teacher shifts from lessons to learning, from classroom management to making connections, you'll sense changes in the way your students respond to you, their classmates, and the partnerships you are building with them. Taking a student-centered approach is not about giving up control of your classroom, but about giving students the opportunity to have some say over *what* and *how* they learn. When students know you are willing to share authority with them, they will consent to your reasonable exercise of authority in the classroom. This consent quietly shifts the classroom dynamic from coercion and resistance to collaboration and shared responsibility. What you will not find in this book is a chapter on classroom management. As your classroom becomes student centered, I predict that if management is currently an issue for you, it won't be any longer. Each student has a unique history, perspective, strengths, and needs. When you take the time to learn their stories, students feel known and trusted and want to learn. They will show you in so many ways they are ready to move forward with their learning and their lives.

In the next chapter, we'll move on to the third student-centered teaching practice: make space for speaking and listening. I discuss how to give your students opportunities to develop their communication skills, as well as the confidence to put those skills to work.

Next Steps for Supporting Personal Growth

The following tool details some steps you can take to foster independence, imagination, and integrity in your classroom. For each step, note the date you tried it and reflect on how it went: What did you do? How did it go? What would you change? What's next? Spaces are available at the end for you to plan additional steps you can take toward a student-centered approach to teaching.

Next Steps Tried	Date Tried	Reflection
During class discussion, encourage students to speak to one another rather than just to you.		
When you ask a question and receive responses from students, say, "Thank you," rather than "That's good" or "That's right."		
Pose "What if . . ." questions to encourage students to exercise their imaginations: What if Earth had two suns? What if we made it illegal to throw anything away? What if $2 + 2 = 5$?		
Encourage students to share observations and experiences that raise ethical questions, and devote some class time to discussing how to deal with them.		

CHAPTER 3

Make Space for Speaking and Listening

The goal of the student-centered classroom is to provide the conditions for each student to engage in active learning. Doing a good job on the units of study and scoring well on standardized tests is not enough. Becoming ready to take an active role in the classroom and in the larger world requires solid communication skills and the confidence to put them to work. Across grade levels and content areas, students need positive experiences as speakers and listeners. In an elementary classroom, it's easier to integrate communication skills into science, social studies, mathematics, and art. However, at the secondary level, it can be tempting to park speaking and listening at the door to English class or forget about them altogether.

However, these skills are not only interdisciplinary but also universal. As human beings, we need communication skills to find the nearest restroom and to reach beyond the moon. That need forms the third student-centered teaching practice: make space for speaking and listening. Whether in fourth grade, French, or physical education, a student-centered approach develops not only knowledge of content but also the skills and confidence to see speaking in public as an opportunity rather than a dreaded obligation. Whether using color tiles to demonstrate the solution to a fraction problem or creating a public service video about how to recycle at school, students need to be sure of their facts. And students need to be confident about these four things.

1. Their thoughts merit clear expression.
2. They can engage and move an audience.
3. They can gather information and generate new ideas.
4. They can understand and appreciate the ideas of others.

There are many ways for a caring, creative teacher to provide low-risk opportunities for students to practice communication skills and build confidence. Instead of limiting the curriculum to what standardized tests cover, include opportunities for students to develop speaking and listening skills and the confidence to use them in the larger contexts of college, the workplace, and community life. Over twenty-five years of teaching, I came up with hundreds of activities for this purpose, and looking back over my own work has been instructive. There are activities that come and go and others that endure. The ones that endure tend to start out as tasks to practice skills, but they are engaging and flexible enough to be worth repeating, and, as students build skills and confidence, what was once just a task becomes the framework for a performance demonstrating student achievement. In the following sections of this chapter and in chapter 4 (page 61), I offer what I found to be the most engaging and enduring of these tasks that can evolve into performances. Flexibility makes them appropriate across content areas and for both elementary and secondary students. Each section focuses on tasks that develop a particular communication skill, but because communication skills overlap and intertwine, the tasks don't attempt to isolate these naturally interrelated skills.

Speech to Facilitate Thought

The members of the Curriculum Study Commission, founded by Walter Loban, dedicated the 1992 Central California Council of Teachers of English (CCCTE) conference to his work. Loban was a University of California, Berkeley, professor, researcher, and theorist, particularly in the field of spoken language. The program dedication reads, "The memory of his rigorous mind, broad vision, gentle nature, and compassionate heart—all in the service of literature and language and of those who teach, learn, and love both—will continue to inspire us" (Curriculum Study Commission, 1992). Loban's work with the Curriculum Study Commission included writing study group papers, the first of which, from 1966, was titled "The Spoken Word and the Integrity of English Instruction." Loban's (1966) research revealed a reciprocal relationship between facility with oral communication and academic success, which I learned about when I had the good fortune to attend the 1991 annual gathering.

It was there I realized that *spoken language* should play an important role in any classroom, especially a student-centered one. Because most students come to school able to talk and listen but need instruction to read and write, the focus even in elementary school tends to be on the latter skills. In secondary school, teachers still expect students to know how to listen, although they may receive explicit instruction on taking lecture notes. Writing is often a means for students to prove they have listened and done the reading. Because oral communication is seldom on standardized tests, talking tends to be regarded at best as a means to other ends and at worst as something teachers should discourage. Loban's (1976) much-quoted statement sums it up: "The curriculum inevitably shrinks to the boundaries of whatever evaluation the schools use" (p. 121). Although Loban made this statement in 1976, it still holds true. Sarah Wike Loyola (2016) taught Spanish for seventeen years to students from middle school to college. What she learned about language teaching is broadly applicable across content areas:

> Through classroom observation, I have seen that some teachers are much more comfortable letting their students take center stage than others. And I have concluded that those teachers who are most comfortable with student-centered classrooms see the greatest linguistic results, have less attrition from one level to the next, and have more students who are engaged and happy. (Loyola, 2016)

Given our limited knowledge of what students in school now will need to know when they embark on careers, one of the best favors teachers can do is to provide opportunities for students to develop strong oral communication skills—skills that will give them the ability to be valuable members of a team, to collaborate effectively on problems and projects too complex to be solved solo, and to be ready to inform and inspire others as leaders. I've heard teachers say, "I'd love to do more with oral communication, but it takes too much time." In my experience, this is time well spent. The time my students spent on oral communication paid off not only in confidence as speakers but in clarity of thought, power of written expression, and facility as readers.

My respect for the power of oral communication comes not just from experience as a teacher but also from the perspective of a student. I remember sitting in a lecture hall with a hundred other students who were taking a summer course on Shakespeare at the University of California, Berkeley, and hearing the voice of the professor tremble as he announced he would be trying something rather unprecedented. He wanted some volunteers to join him at the lectern to read a scene from one of the plays *aloud*. The dynamics of the room altered instantly, as half a dozen of us made our way to the front of the hall, joined the professor's solo voice, and the words of the play came alive.

The setup of that Berkeley lecture hall is replicated in far too many school classrooms, the long rows of desks and the lectern at the front, putting the emphasis on taking notes rather than making meaning. However, there are ways to integrate oral communication in the classroom. The following sections include strategies that foster speaking skills through group talk, role playing, and choral reading.

Group Talk

In a teacher-directed setting, a student could go all day without saying a word to anyone. The quiet student can simply defer to the teacher and to classmates who like or need to talk. We all have a right to decide whether it's our time to be silent or to make noise, but the act of putting our thoughts not just in words but in *spoken words* is so important that there's quite a bit of brain space devoted to this particular human endeavor. Imaging technology has made it possible for scientists to learn that regions in every major part of the brain, including frontal, parietal, occipital, and temporal lobes, and the cerebellum, are involved in understanding and producing language. Broca's region, in particular, transforms thought into speech (Abbott, 2016).

In chapter 1 (page 11), I offer detailed discussion of the work that goes on in groups in a student-centered classroom. Here I just want to offer one activity and emphasize that group talk is not a side effect of group work; *it's the primary reason for it.*

As a class activity, invite students to write down half a dozen or so questions they would like others to ask them on the worksheet in figure 3.1. The questions can range from "What is your favorite color?" to "What's the hardest thing you've ever had to do?" The questions should, of course, be appropriate for a classroom setting.

The purposes of this activity are to get better acquainted with the members of your class and to increase your awareness of the importance of listening carefully to what other people have to say. Start by writing half a dozen or so questions on the worksheet that you would like your partner to ask you. Then, trade worksheets with your partner, and interview each other using the questions. Listen carefully and make notes on the worksheet. Trade worksheets again so you and your partner can check the accuracy of each other's notes. Sometimes what we think we heard isn't what was actually said! Trade back, and use your notes to introduce your partner to the class.

Questions you would like your partner to ask you	Your partner's notes on your answers

---

Figure 3.1: Worksheet for paired interviews.

*Visit **go.SolutionTree.com/instruction** for a free reproducible version of this figure.*

It's important that the questions are truly ones that each student would like to be asked, so it's probably wise to avoid providing a list for students to choose from. On the other hand, it might loosen things up to give students a few minutes to come up with a question or two and then go around the class to sample and share just one question. Then give students time to finish their lists of questions. When each student has a list of questions, randomly pair students, and ask them to trade worksheets and interview each other using the questions on their partners' worksheets. Encourage students to listen carefully to each other and to make notes. When both partners have been interviewed, they can trade worksheets again and check the accuracy of each other's notes. Finally, ask the partners to introduce each other to the class using what they learned during the interviews.

Putting thoughts into spoken words is hard. But the work gets easier—and more fun—with practice. From group talk comes growing individual student confidence that the words will be there when needed in the classroom and in the larger world.

Role Playing

Elementary students are typically uninhibited about taking on the role of a hungry puffin or a grizzly bear munching clover. Secondary students are slower to get out of their seats for role playing. In both cases, it's important that students have background information to draw on. They should know something about the situation they'll be dramatizing and also about the lives of people who might be involved. An invitation to *imagine talk*, such as what might occur among members of a Guatemalan family fearful of separation or strangers in Hong Kong meeting for the first time at a protest march, stimulates the process of putting thought into spoken words.

The first time you initiate role play, it might get things moving to prepare some 3 x 5 cards ahead of time. On one side, briefly describe a situation that would already be familiar to students, and, on the other side, list five people who might be present at the scene. Give group members a little time to talk their situation and characters over, and then offer them a worksheet to help them prepare, like the example in figure 3.2 (page 44).

Once students get some experience setting up a scene and creating characters, they can do the real heavy lifting, which is to decide on a situation with dramatic potential. With some preparation, students at all levels can simulate a courtroom, a city council chamber, a press conference with astronauts just returned from space—any important contemporary or historical moment can come to life in the classroom through role playing. With background information and some role-play practice, secondary students can develop original role plays on currently trending or controversial topics. Informal role-playing activities prepare students to write, rehearse, and present a more formal type of role playing called choral reading.

Details of the situation: Imagine a specific place and time of day. What simple items could your group include in the role play that would help define place and time?	
Your character: Who is your character, and how do they feel about the situation? How can your character make the situation better? Worse?	
Standard behavior: What would your character usually say and do in this situation? What would really surprise one or more of the other characters?	
Key line: What is the most important thing your character can say to solve the problem, correct misunderstandings, improve relationships, or express true feelings?	
Props: What simple items could your character carry, wear, or use that would help make the character believable and interesting?	

Figure 3.2: Role play guidelines.

*Visit **go.SolutionTree.com/instruction** for a free reproducible version of this figure.*

Choral Reading

Strictly defined, *choral reading*, or unison reading, is reading aloud together with the whole class or group (Reading Rockets, n.d.). It is a strategy that helps students gain confidence in their ability to decode, pronounce words correctly, and convey understanding of what they are reading aloud, using pace, tone, and inflection. Typically, a small group of students will read a short text aloud with their teacher, who models appropriate pace and correct pronunciation. You can see a video example of this at www.reading rockets.org/strategies/choral_reading, which is narrated by Joanne Meier (Reading Rockets, n.d.), the research director of Reading Rockets. In the video, a first-grade teacher demonstrates how to get the most out of a story with dialogue and then invites her students to read in unison with her. But there is much more to be done with choral reading once students have been introduced to it.

A choral reading can be done with an original composition as well as with a published text. Either way, the power of multiple voices to make a sequence of lines come to life in the classroom is immense yet, at the same time, intuitive. When a colleague asked me to show her students how to do a choral reading, I began by distributing copies of a choral-reading script and asking for volunteers to do a sight reading. Even though the students were reading the lines for the first time and had no chance to rehearse, the dynamic of their multiple voices was amazing. And my colleague's students immediately understood the enticing nature of the opportunity.

Since students just need to see an example of a choral-reading script and experiment with performing it to get what choral reading is about, they can begin working on their own choral readings without much additional coaching. Students' thoughtfully written, carefully rehearsed, and expressively performed choral readings will make the hairs stand up on the back of your neck. Choral readings have the power to get right to the heart of matters, using spoken language to create an experience that is meaningful and moving.

You can draw scripts for choral readings from course texts and related materials. Individuals and groups can bring in texts that interest them and compose original scripts. Once students know what a choral-reading script looks like, all that's left is to suggest some ways they can take the project further than the sample script. For example, they can use voices like instruments to achieve a particular effect: high or deep, soft or loud, staccato or sustained, solo or unison. They will quickly figure out how to indicate voice dynamics on the script by using italics, bold, capital letters, and so on. Each group needs enough class time to practice so all members know their script well, come in promptly on cue, and pronounce words correctly and confidently. They must articulate each word of each line clearly, expressively, and with appropriate emphasis. Students can perform in a row at the front of the room, from the corners of the room, or from shifting perspectives as they move through the room. For elementary students, I've included tips from Poetry Out Loud (n.d.) with age-appropriate modifications (see figure 3.3, page 46).

The guidelines in figure 3.4 (page 46) are adapted from Poetry Out Loud (n.d.) evaluation criteria. These criteria set a high standard, but it is one that secondary students can meet because they're so invested in the choral reading.

The example in figure 3.5 (page 47) is a choral reading written after students had read *The Things They Carried*, novelist Tim O'Brien's (1990) book about his experience serving in the military in Vietnam.

The choral reading was written by a student named Mike Henss. When I got in touch with Mike to request his permission to include his choral reading in this book, he was initially concerned that work he had done as a sixteen-year-old would not hold up for him as an adult. But when he reread the choral reading, he found that it still captured how much O'Brien's (1990) book meant to him:

> I have only a vague memory of completing this assignment, but I do have very fond memories of reading *The Things They Carried*. I actually purchased a used copy of this book last year to keep around in the event that I feel the need to reread a chapter or two (or more). Truth

> Put a check mark next to each item that describes you as a choral reader. It's OK to leave some items blank. The purpose of the checklist is to celebrate your strengths and figure out what you need to work on.
>
> ☐ Before the performance, make sure you know how to pronounce each word correctly.
>
> ☐ Stand up straight, and try to make eye contact with the audience.
>
> ☐ Speak clearly, slowly, and loudly enough so the audience understands each word.
>
> ☐ Pay close attention to the script so you are ready to speak when it's your turn.
>
> ☐ Speak your lines with feeling that fits with the message of your script.

Source: Adapted from Poetry Out Loud, n.d.

Figure 3.3: Choral-reading performance guidelines for elementary students.

*Visit **go.SolutionTree.com/instruction** for a free reproducible version of this figure.*

> On the scale of 1 to 4, 1 indicates more practice is needed while 4 indicates your practice has produced strong performance skills. Use this checklist several times. The first time, your purpose is to get familiar with the guidelines. The second time, your purpose is to figure out where you are strong and where you need more practice. The final time is to celebrate your performance!
>
> ① ② ③ ④
> **Physical Presence**—Ease and comfort with the audience. Engagement with the audience through physical presence, including appropriate body language and confidence—without appearing artificial.
>
> ① ② ③ ④
> **Voice and Articulation**—All words pronounced correctly, and the projection, rhythm, and intonation greatly enhance the recitation. Pacing appropriate to the script.
>
> ① ② ③ ④
> **Evidence of Understanding**—The message of the script is powerfully and clearly conveyed to the audience. The performance captures meaning, themes, allusions, irony, tone, and other nuances.
>
> ① ② ③ ④
> **Overall Performance**—The script and performance captivate the audience.

Source: Adapted from Poetry Out Loud, n.d.

Figure 3.4: Choral-reading performance guidelines for secondary students.

*Visit **go.SolutionTree.com/instruction** for a free reproducible version of this figure.*

Reader 1 Courage	Reader 2 Violence	Reader 3 Social pressures
1 The threat	1 The power	3 Becomes routine
2 Of death	2 Of the Vietnamese	All DEATH AND DESTRUCTION
3 And destruction	3 Was underestimated	
1 Struggling	All VIOLENCE	1 Friends being
2 Connects	1 From 1968	2 Killed
3 The lives	2 To 1972	3 Villages
1 Of people	3 Tim O'Brien	1 Wasted
2 And their experiences	1 Served in	2 Land
3 Setting	2 The war	3 Destroyed
1 And imagery	3 He received	All SORROW
2 Make the book	1 A Purple Heart	1 True war stories
3 Alive	2 For his efforts	2 Are never
All VIETNAM	3 And was	3 About war
1 Changed	1 Honorably discharged	1 True war stories
2 The lives	All SOCIAL PRESSURES	2 Are never
3 Of many	2 Marijuana smoking	3 About war

Source: © 1996 by Mike Henss. Used with permission.

Figure 3.5: Choral-reading student example based on *The Things They Carried*.

be told, this was the first time that I felt compelled to read a book so thoroughly and so briskly, as the short stories within it contained adult themes that were imbued with a sense of gravitas that was impossible for me to ignore. (M. Henss, personal communication, April 27, 2020)

Mike's comment is a reminder that no assignment is an end in itself. What matters is what that sixteen-year-old takes away from it. Mike makes it clear that his takeaway was one of the things teachers most hope for: deep, enduring engagement in an important book.

Students can compose choral readings using a wide variety of resources: material quoted verbatim from a novel, historical speeches, course notes, and contemporary texts such as song lyrics and film dialogue. Students can create choral readings that comment on a big question such as, "What is valuable?" or a contemporary issue. Students can generate choral readings using figures of historical or literary importance to speak with one another across time and space. The versatility of the form is part of what makes it so engaging. Feedback from my students consistently identified the opportunity to compose and perform choral readings as a highlight of the class.

Group talk, role playing, and choral reading are all useful strategies to encourage productive talk in class. Students must also be mindful of how others will hear their words. In the next section, I'll discuss how to write and speak for listeners, which in turn develops students' own capacity to listen.

Enhanced Listening Through Writing and Speaking

How actively or passively we perceive the world is going to have an impact on how large or small that world is. This is especially true of what we perceive by listening. A summary of the benefits of strong listening skills that are identified in multiple sources shows that these benefits have the potential for a significant impact not only on a student's academic success but on all aspects of life (Waterford.org, 2020).

- Greater ability to communicate
- Faster second language acquisition
- Lower levels of frustration, anxiety, and depression
- Improved relationship skills
- Stronger sense of empathy

According to Harvard's Usable Knowledge (2017) research initiative, active listening is a sign of respect. When one student listens carefully to another, it's mute evidence of appreciation not only of what the speaker has to say but also of what the listener can learn from other students. Active listening "reinforces the value of coming prepared, thinking independently, listening carefully, and working as a team—as one student picks up where another hits a wall" (Usable Knowledge, 2017).

In this section, you will find two highly engaging exercises that inspire students to write and speak to capture and hold the attention of listeners. These strategies also give the audience members opportunities to listen so well you can hear the proverbial pin drop. The first exercise is the occasional paper, and the second is a short speech that helps students develop effective timing.

Occasional Paper

In the article "A Writing Assignment / A Way of Life," former teacher and high school English department chair Bill Martin (2003) describes the *occasional paper* as an informal essay anchored in observations of daily life. Once my students began writing occasional papers, or *OPs* as they were fondly known, they did indeed become both a writing assignment and a way of life in our classroom. I would participate as well by offering my own OPs. My students wrote OPs about writing utensil preference, the community mail art project PostSecret (https://postsecret.com), switching roles with one's twin, Humpty Dumpty, National Novel Writing Month, and toilets that flush automatically, to name just a few. Writing OPs provides an opportunity not just to share observations but also to become conscious of ways to shape a story so it conveys attitude, achieves the desired impact on the reader, and ends with a lesson or moral. But the most important role OPs play is helping students *listen*. Students must listen carefully to the sounds of the world they live in as they become acute observers of it, and they must listen carefully to one another. OPs exist primarily as spoken language, read aloud in class just once. As the year goes on and presentations of OPs become a regular part of the class, unexpected topics and original stylistic touches rub off, and students grow tremendously as writers, speakers, and listeners, being careful to catch every fascinating word. When implementing an OP assignment, it's important to use a flexible due date and assessment, write with students, urge students to stay with a topic, and be willing to take risks.

Use a Flexible Due Date and Assessment

Following Martin's (2003) recommendations, the due date for an OP is flexible and the paper is *not* turned in. The most important assessment students receive is the collective gasp or howl of laughter or awed "Wow!" from their classmates, which might just be the most powerful confidence builder of all. Brainstorm possible topics with elementary students, invite them to write and present an OP on their own or with a partner, and give them time to share and comment on what they liked. The range of possible topics is unlimited (except by respect for others). Invite students to focus on occasions when they notice something in the larger world that is related to course material: putting forensic ecology to work on a polluted creek or applying principles of statistics to a local election, for example. Just be sure to leave students room to make choices. Figure 3.6 (page 50) provides OP guidelines for elementary students. For secondary students, you can provide more formal guidelines (see figure 3.7, page 50) and enter credit for a good-faith effort.

The desire to earn the respect of their peers is a strong motivator for teenagers (Gopnik, 2012). For the few who might try to slide by, the best response is giving them the opportunity to try again. If necessary, with secondary students, I'll give a sliding-by presentation twenty-five of a possible fifty points; then, it's clear to the student that the OP is important, and a half-hearted effort won't do. Once the OP becomes part of the class culture, points are irrelevant because students love presenting and hearing them so much. Over the course of two or three rounds of OPs, students pick up new strategies, deepen their appreciation of their classmates, and broaden their understanding of both the foolishness and the sweetness of the world we inhabit.

> Your occasional paper (or OP) can be about anything you have noticed in the world around you that you think your classmates will think is interesting, surprising, or even amazing.
> - ☐ Brainstorm a list of possible topics with your class, a partner, or on your own.
> - ☐ Select a topic, and write what you have noticed about it. Be sure to include details you think no one else may notice unless you point them out.
> - ☐ Your OP can be serious or funny. Just be sure it's respectful of other people.
> - ☐ Make a copy of your OP that is easy to read, and practice reading it aloud.
> - ☐ Read your OP to a partner, small group, or your class.
> - ☐ Listen carefully when your classmates read their OPs, and let them know what you liked. You might also get some good ideas for how to write your next OP.

Figure 3.6: Occasional paper guidelines for elementary students.

*Visit **go.SolutionTree.com/instruction** for a free reproducible version of this figure.*

Things to avoid	Things to do
Attacks on an individual or divulging information about an individual that should be kept in confidence	Explore the details of an occasion that would usually be dismissed as unimportant
Formulaic organization (five-paragraph essay approach)	Let the paper grow naturally from ideas and purpose
A paper that is brief, undeveloped, or lacks detail	Blend description, narrative, and explanation to engage the audience
Use of generic phrases or clichés, and reliance on sweeping generalizations	Write the OP so it sounds like you're speaking
Grammatical or usage errors	Break the rules for effect
Reading the paper for the first time in class or trying to read from a handwritten draft	Practice reading the paper aloud before reading it in class, and read from a typed, double-spaced script

Figure 3.7: Occasional paper guidelines for secondary students.

*Visit **go.SolutionTree.com/instruction** for a free reproducible version of this figure.*

Toward the end of the year, there are often some lovely homage OPs that comment on what individual students shared.

Write With Students

When students asked me to do an OP for them, I searched for a topic—one that would be utterly true and central to my own experience in life, yet appealing to them—just as they searched for what would engage their audience. Students had shared fears, hopes, solemn moments, and moments of hilarity. My OP had to be just as honest and courageous as theirs. Fortunately, a topic found me. When I performed "The Hallmark Factory," about a New Year's greeting card tradition my husband and I have, my students knew I was sharing from the heart.

> ### Occasional Paper: The Hallmark Factory
>
> On the summer solstice, my husband and I will celebrate our thirty-sixth year of marriage. There are two important things that have kept our relationship going. The first is we agree about the principles by which we live our lives. The second is that we have sustained the ability to surprise one another. A couple of days ago, my husband said, "You've got to see this," and clicked through half a dozen images in his camera that looked like shots of a canyon wall striated into uneven horizontal bands of geologic history.
>
> "What am I looking at?" I asked.
>
> With a twinkle in his eye, he led me to a large sheet of tempered glass flat on the ground next to the garage. "I dropped my hammer on it," he said, "and then snapped those pictures."
>
> When I looked closely, I realized that the canyon wall I thought I saw in his photos was there before me in the fractured glass.
>
> "Listen," he said, "it's still breaking."
>
> I heard a kind of rustle, a sound more of restlessness than of breaking, and, as I watched fascinated, the striations spread further and further toward the corners of the pane of glass. He had broken it on a tarp in preparation for safely discarding it but wanted to capture the event.
>
> "This," he said, with an arm around my shoulders, "might be our next card."
>
> Each year, he contributes an image and I contribute a poem to the New Year's greeting card we send to family and friends. It's a collaboration that literally gives us a chance to work together on a project and figuratively represents the creative give-and-take of our long marriage. Sometimes the image drives the poem, and sometimes the poem drives the image. The collaboration required to operate our "Hallmark factory" gives us the opportunities to surprise and delight one another that keep an old marriage young at heart.

Urge Students to Stay With a Topic

Giving students choices about their topics and approaches might sometimes include encouraging a student to stay with a topic for a while. There's no need for every project to focus on a new topic if a current one—or some aspect of it—still matters to the student. For example, my OP could lead in as many directions as that sheet of breaking glass, developing into researched nonfiction or a letter to the editor. Always jumping from one topic to another can be exhausting, while staying with a topic rich enough to reward sustained exploration can be deeply satisfying.

Be Willing to Take Risks

I remember a student presenting an OP about teaching his father the protocols of the men's restroom to uproarious laughter, and I remember a student whose mother was dying of cancer sharing an OP about shopping at the supermarket, knowing she must take on the responsibilities that her mother would never be able to shoulder again and longing to retreat to a time when her mother did the shopping and she was just a girl who knew nothing of sickness and grief. As she took us with her up and down the aisles of her life, we shared her burden for a while, and she learned something about her own strength from the tears welling in our eyes. Both students were willing to take risks because they knew their audience well and were absolutely confident their peers would appreciate and value their experiences and the skills they used to convey them. Experiences like these in turn serve as powerful motivators to provide a classroom where students can share what really matters to them and know it will be safe, even satisfying, to do so.

Short Speech

The informality of OPs prepares students for writing and presenting a slightly more formal short speech, an activity that manages to encompass an impressive number of instructional strategies. In *Classroom Instruction That Works*, coauthors Robert J. Marzano, Debra J. Pickering, and Jane E. Pollock (2001) identify nine research-based strategies that increase student achievement. The chart in figure 3.8 shows where each of these strategies contributes to the process of creating a short speech.

Speaking in front of the class is a worthy challenge for many students. For elementary students, one minute is a doable length for a short speech (Finney & Giansante, n.d.). For secondary students, a three-minute limit allows enough time to develop an idea and requires students to edit carefully. The Three Minute Thesis (3MT) competition memorably demonstrated the three-minute limit. Launched in 2008 by the University of Queensland (n.d.) in Australia, the competition gave graduate students an opportunity to present their research as long as they could figure out how to do it well in three minutes. Why three minutes? This was a period of drought in Queensland, during which people kept three-minute egg timers in the bathroom to limit their showers (University of Queensland, n.d.). If you could have a good shower in three minutes, a good speech should be possible in the same amount of time.

Instructional strategy	Short speech process
1. Identifying similarities and differences	Develop a position on a topic.
2. Summarizing and note taking	Gather information.
3. Reinforcing effort and recognition	Get feedback from the teacher on topic and approach.
4. Utilizing homework and practice	Create a working draft and begin reading the draft aloud to see how it works as a speech.
5. Making nonlinguistic representations	Develop a poster or slide show to introduce or illustrate the speech.
6. Using cooperative learning	Check in with collaborative group members about how the process is going.
7. Setting objectives and providing feedback	Listen to group members practice their speeches and provide feedback.
8. Generating and testing hypotheses	Consider the possibility that the process may have modified or altered the original position.
9. Employing cues, questions, and advance organizers	Use worksheets provided by the teacher to prepare for presentation and reflection.

Source: Adapted from Marzano et al., 2001.

Figure 3.8: Employing student achievement strategies for the process of creating a short speech.

In practice, the three-minute speech not only gives secondary students enough time to make a significant point but it's also short enough to make it feasible for an entire class to present speeches in just a few class meetings. Early in the year, students can share something they know how to do that might surprise even those who know them well. For example, a natural how-to speech for many students is a family tradition related to their cultural background. Secondary students enjoy presenting how-to speeches that include a subtext of social commentary, for example, how to order at Starbucks or how to prepare for the prom on a budget. When students are feeling more comfortable giving a speech, the topics can become more academic. Converting existing work into a short speech gives students an opportunity to focus on what makes a speech different from a lab report or an essay. And staying with an idea helps students feel they really know something about themselves and the world we live in. If internet access is available, students can use a video or audio clip to illustrate the speech. If you offer this option, students also need an opportunity to check their equipment beforehand to prevent the frustration of a link not working or the school's website filter blocking a webpage.

To guide students through the process of developing and presenting their short speeches, teachers should help them attend to micro-revision, timing, the speech's sequence and feedback, and the audience experience.

Micro-Revision

Revising existing work into a short speech is likely to require cutting some material. This should be a "no pain, no gain" process for students, one that challenges them to weigh the value of each word, statistic, and example. *Micro-revision* also helps students focus on their audience and how to apply lessons learned from presenting OPs and choral readings to make their speeches lively and memorable.

Timing

Once students have done the hard work of cutting their speeches down to the age-appropriate limits—one minute for elementary students and three minutes for secondary students—invite several students to practice presenting to the class. These students tend to rush through their speeches because they may not have cut enough material to present at an audience-friendly pace. Once students realize the disservice that rushing through their presentations does to their ideas, wit, and well-crafted writing, the teacher can offer an additional thirty seconds to one minute. Be sure to tell them, "Don't add anything, but use the extra time to do a good job with the presentation." You will probably get a big sigh of relief, and students will get the message that the additional time is to make their deliveries as lively and memorable as their content. The extra time shifts the focus from *what* students say to *how* they say it and provides opportunities for them to review their spoken language skills and gain focused practice. Editing the original essay to fit the time limit can be difficult, but the concise, lively prose that results is worth it. The example in figure 3.9 shows what kind of thoughtful, engaged pieces students can produce for a three-minute speech. Although the speech begins as a written argument that includes both a bibliography and reflective commentary, for presentation, the speaker integrates acknowledgement of sources into the text of the speech.

> **DADT: Don't Ask, Don't Tell? Or Discrimination and Differences Today?**
>
> In 1863, the Emancipation Proclamation freed the slaves.
>
> In 1920, women gained the right to vote after years of protesting and fighting by suffragettes.
>
> It seems like, for perhaps the first time, everyone is truly free.
>
> Well . . . almost everyone, that is. Restrictions are still present, and they come *straight*, excuse the pun, from our own military.
>
> In the year 2010, men *and* women of all ethnicities can fight in the army. It is *open* to all . . . except *open*ly gay homosexuals. One main part of the policy reads, "The presence in the armed forces of persons who demonstrate a propensity or intent to engage in homosexual acts would create an unacceptable risk to the high standards of morale, good order and discipline, and unit cohesion that are the essence of military capability."
>
> In some cases, it's hard not to recognize that they have a valid point. In this day and age, gays are still not considered equal in many people's minds. Though support of homosexuals appears to be on the rise in many areas, homosexuality itself is in no way commonly accepted. Homosexual marriages are only performed in five states, excluding California where a ruling is pending. In fact, California is a very interesting case because of its apparent indecisiveness on the issue. First it was allowed, then it was banned, then the ban was lifted. They're the Brett Favre of gay marriage; they can't make up their minds.
>
> To many people, the word *homosexual* carries numerous negative stereotypes. Gay men, the majority of those the policy affects, are "flamboyant." They talk in high and "lispy" voices and all around act womanly. They are called *faggots* and *queers*.
>
> Now, returning to the aforementioned quote from the policy, it's obvious that the army's "high standards of morale" and its "good order" would be thrown into turmoil if open homosexuals were allowed in the army. Says one soldier, "I want to know my buddies will cover my ass . . . not just stare at it!" Certainly, many of his fellow soldiers would echo his view . . . right?
>
> Wrong. His view would hold water if it wasn't for the fact that the DADT policy in no way prevents gays from joining the military. It just says that they cannot be open about it. Lieutenant Colonel Joe Wallis says, "Most of us know a number of homosexuals serving with us and respect them for their professionalism and work ethic." Another soldier who is simply identified as "JD" claims that he has lived most of his military career completely open with his comrades, simply not disclosing the info to his superiors, and "never encountered any trouble."
>
> If what they say is true, then what is the point of banning homosexuality in the army anyway? There are plenty of closeted homosexuals in the military, we know that. Since the Clinton Administration made DADT official U.S. policy on February 28, 1994, the military has discharged over thirteen thousand soldiers.
>
> How can the military argue that the very presence of open homosexuals would "create an unacceptable risk" when there are already closeted gays who are getting by without creating a disturbance?

Figure 3.9: Example of written script for short speech. continued ▶

> What immediate dangers will be brought on by allowing gays to enter the military? What is the harm of giving them a chance, letting people be open about who they are? If, in doing so, it turns out that gays are a great bane to our military, that the greatest fears of DADT's supporters come to fruition, then by all means put the DADT policy back in place . . .
>
> But until that happens, when there is no proof that anything bad will happen at all and evidence actually points to homosexuals doing nothing but good for the military, it is the policy itself that is the true blight of our armed forces. At the very least, they could start with just one branch and move forward from there. Initiate it first in the Coast Guard, and if all goes well, expand it to include the Navy, or any of the other branches. As time goes by, and if all goes well, eventually the entire military would be free of segregation and the controversy that goes with it.

Source: © 2010 by Luke Shearin. Used with permission.

Presentation Sequence and Feedback

If the teacher organizes the presentation sequence and feedback in advance, the day of presentations will run more smoothly. Figure 3.10 shows an example of a form to use for student feedback. Make enough copies of the feedback form so each student receives three. Ask students to write their name next to "Presenter's name" on the forms and then fold them and place them in a basket. Once all sheets are in, pass the basket around the class so each student can draw three forms, checking that they do not draw their own or more than one form for the same person. This is a simple process, yet even secondary students love drawing the forms and opening them to see who will receive their feedback.

Student feedback on speech

Presenter's name: _____

☐ Regular eye contact   ☐ Expressive use of language
☐ Alert posture   ☐ Interesting ideas
☐ Ear-friendly pacing   ☐ Appropriate word choice
☐ Clear, audible voice   ☐ Engaging style

Comment on what you liked most about the presentation:

Comment written by _____

Figure 3.10: Student-feedback form for presentations.

*Visit **go.SolutionTree.com/instruction** for a free reproducible version of this figure.*

Teachers expect students to be a courteous audience to all presenters; students know they must listen especially carefully to the speeches of those whose forms they drew for feedback. Early in the year, the teacher could collect and review the student-feedback forms before distributing them to the presenters. However, I found that I could trust students to provide the kind of feedback they would like to receive. I also completed a feedback form for each student as he or she was presenting, but I saved my notes to share with each student later. I wanted to send a clear message that what the presenter's peers have to say is valuable.

Audience Experience

Some students have formal audience experiences (through dramatic and musical performances), while the informality of a sporting event or a battle of the bands can influence others' understanding of audience protocol. Because the room where presentations are taking place is simultaneously a classroom and a stage, even a student well acquainted with formal audience conduct might shuffle through his or her backpack while a presentation is in progress, unaware of the distraction it creates. A normally polite student coming into the classroom after getting a drink of water might walk right in front of the presenter. I always tried to head off awkward moments by asking students to imagine disruptions *before* they happened and then conduct themselves so such moments didn't occur.

Teachers may feel there just isn't enough time to focus on the importance of speaking and listening skills, but these are the tools people use to find truth and speak truth to injustice. It takes great courage to speak out when everyone else is going along with the program. The work you and your students do in a student-centered environment will prepare them for standardized testing, but you should not limit what you offer them to what is on such tests. What matters much more is for students to achieve the communication skills, deepen the understanding, and build the confidence to make their voices heard.

The discussion of how to enhance communication skills continues in the next chapter, where we'll tackle the fourth student-centered teaching practice: deepen understanding with writing and reading. You can help students understand their own lives and the lives of others through attention to the processes of writing and reading.

Next Steps for Making Space for Speaking and Listening

The following tool details some steps you can take to experiment with speaking and listening in your classroom. For each step, note the date you tried it and reflect on how it went: What did you do? How did it go? What would you change? What's next? There are spaces available at the end for you to plan additional steps you can take toward a student-centered approach to teaching.

Next Steps Tried	Date Tried	Reflection
Ask students to be as quiet as possible for five minutes. During this time, they should listen carefully and write down what they hear in the room. Then ask students to share one of the things they heard.		
In groups, ask students to talk about who they enjoy listening to—musician, actor, real-life hero, friend, family member, and so on. Then ask them to write down two or three things about the way this person performs or speaks that makes them want to listen. Ask each group to share.		
Brainstorm with students about the *what ifs* of public speaking: What if you stumble over a word? What if you get nervous and go too fast? What if the audience doesn't laugh at something you meant to be funny? What if they do laugh when you don't expect them to? What if they yawn or fidget? What if they aren't interested in your topic?		
Write a short speech about some aspect of your life that is not obvious to your students. Before presenting, ask students to give you advice to help you do a good job with your presentation. Then present your speech, following their advice.		

Next Steps Tried	Date Tried	Reflection

CHAPTER 4

Deepen Understanding With Writing and Reading

The fourth student-centered teaching practice, deepen understanding with writing and reading, requires stepping back and remembering when the letters on a page first came to life in your mind, and what it was like to shape letters and make words that another person could understand. Writing and reading are not just skills; they are powerful, life-changing acts that teachers should not shackle to rote academic tasks. Moffett and Wagner (1992) do not mince words about the damage teachers can do by using writing primarily to test reading comprehension:

> School writing has been too much just a testing instrument of the reading. And the "marking" of papers in the name of evaluation has made generations of students hate to write even so much as a personal letter later in life and probably accounts, more than any factors of intrinsic difficulty, for the poor writing ability of most high school graduates. Likewise, constant testing for reading comprehension by oral or written questions makes students feel punished for reading. (p. 242)

These words are nearly thirty years old, but they continue to ring true. Instead of using writing to test reading comprehension, help students see writing as a way to deepen their engagement in and understanding of their own lives.

Beth Pandolpho (2018) is a teacher resource specialist for curriculum and instruction and the author of the 2020 book *I'm Listening: How Teacher-Student Relationships Improve Reading, Writing, Speaking, and Listening.* She advocates restoring reading and writing to catalysts of student self-expression. Giving students some freedom in what they read and write about is a great way to tap into their inner lives and draw them into true engagement. Pandolpho (2018) writes:

> I want my students to understand that their ideas can bring about change, so I work to give them choices to write about topics they feel passionate about. They ask probing questions and devote the time necessary to develop a compelling argument, meticulously craft sentences, and carefully choose their words.

The teacher can also serve as a model to aspire to. Instead of assigning a chapter and giving a pop quiz, help students understand what goes on in the minds of experienced readers. In *Rigorous Reading*, Nancy Frey and Douglas Fisher (2013) offer advice about how teachers can model their reading process for students: "Modeling is a time when you highlight the areas that you predict will be difficult for students, and you show them how you resolve comprehension problems" (Frey & Fisher, 2013, p. 27). Teachers can show students how to interact with complex text. Depending on the level of complexity in question, an expert reader activates different processes, and allowing students to observe this is a valuable tool in the classroom (Frey & Fisher, 2013).

This chapter suggests ways to infuse writing with meaning and joy by using it for multiple purposes and ways to illuminate the process of reading by sharing what goes on in the minds of those who love to read with those who aren't yet sure.

Achievement of Multiple Purposes With Writing

At the beginning of each school year, I would distribute a survey to my classes as a first step to get to know my students. In it I asked for one thing they'd like to change about English class. Often the response is something like this: "Please could we write something besides analytical essays?" It's important that students know how to approach an academic writing task, whether it's literary analysis or a lab report. But writing is too powerful a medium to limit it to academic tasks. Writing provides students with ways to organize and develop their thoughts, to record and come to grips with important moments in their lives, to communicate about matters ranging from the pragmatic to the impassioned. This chapter includes sections on researched narratives and letters to the editor, both of which help students develop essential skills at the same time that they encourage students to view writing as an engaging form of expression rather than an academic chore.

Researched Narratives

Researched narratives start with stories that emerge from personal experience. Students make a natural transition from narrative to research when they look for additional information to add detail and depth to their stories. The idea that a single piece of writing could both tell a story and include research can be a game changer for students who are sure they hate academic writing. There are many ways to achieve this, starting with provisional writing.

Provisional Writing

Much of the writing teachers ask students to do should be for the purpose of thinking about something. This is where *provisional writing* comes in. According to educator and author Dave Stuart Jr. (2017), "Provisional writing is only for the purpose of learning. It does not need to communicate to anyone but oneself. This would include written warm-ups, written exit tickets—even notes based on reading or listening activities."

When we write down what we're thinking, a dialogue begins between our thoughts and the words on the paper, which deepens both thinking and writing. Provisional writing like this—practicing a stylistic device, working through an idea, reflecting on a class activity—is a useful strategy. It gives teachers an opportunity to introduce material, teach minilessons, share information, and develop skills without asking students to invest more time or energy than necessary. Students can share passages from their provisional writing with the class to everyone's benefit, but there's no need for students to turn in their writing for grading. The work serves its provisional purpose and can remain in the students' notebooks as part of the evidence students gather to demonstrate progress toward achievement of learning goals.

Process Writing

On the other hand, when teachers ask students to spend time with a piece of writing, taking it through a collaborative process and multiple drafts, they're engaging in *process writing*. In process writing, students should be partners in decisions about topic and approach. My students wrote about everything from failing to save a drowning bird and crashing onto a rock because Dad didn't use the right knot for the tire swing to learning to manage stress through yoga and hiking a section of the Appalachian Trail in a program that required leaving behind shampoo and deodorant as well as a cell phone. Especially for students who are convinced that school writing can't be fun, process writing reassures everyone that the first step is a simple narrative and just a page or so is a good length to start with. As an example, I described for students what it's like to watch hungry deer looking for food and making a trail through deep winter snow (figure 4.1, page 64).

For elementary students, there's a wealth of narrative nonfiction that would work as models for their own. For example, students could experience *This Is How We Do It: One Day in the Lives of Seven Kids From Around the World* by author, illustrator, and animator Matt Lamothe (2017), and then respond with comparable details from a day in their own lives.

Once students have written their stories, the next step is for them to do a little background research to help them add detail and heighten the credibility of their work. The first time they work with researched narrative, limit the number of sources so the students' focus remains on the story. For example, you might ask students to use no more than one or two sources (instead of requiring a minimum number). The story remains the focus, but the addition of facts from a couple of sources heightens its credibility (see figure 4.2, page 64).

> The herd of deer is getting bigger. They circle the house, searching for that last twig, stripping the bark from saplings. I want to help, but I'm pretty sure you're not supposed to feed them because it can make things worse. So I watch. There's a route they follow that takes them over the ridge behind our house, into the neighbor's woods, and back again. As time passes, I can see a narrow trail etched in the snow. I want to walk along that trail. One afternoon when the deer are in the woods, I plunge into the snow, sinking at every step until I reach the deer trail, darkened with deer poop. The repeated passing of the herd along the narrow path has broken through and compacted the snow, and the pellets of poop have composted into a kind of sand, giving their narrow hooves traction. As the going becomes easier, I understand how the deer can break into a run, white tails flashing, without breaking their legs. I follow the trail across the face of the ridge. It's too cold to stay out long. As I turn to retrace my steps, I pause to look from this new perspective at the window where I had sat and watched the deer and would sit and watch again.

Figure 4.1: Initial narrative—Hungry deer.

> The herd of deer gathers in ever larger numbers as their hunger grows. This is a survival strategy called *yarding* (Wiley & Hulsey, n.d.). They circle the house, searching for that last twig, stripping the bark from saplings. I want to help, but you're not supposed to feed them because it can make things worse. If their bellies fill up with food they can't digest, they starve (Johnson, 2018). So I watch. There's a route they follow that takes them over the ridge behind our house, into the neighbor's woods, and back again. As time passes, I can see a narrow trail etched in the snow. I want to walk along that trail. One afternoon when the deer are in the woods, I plunge into the snow, sinking at every step until I reach the deer trail, darkened with scat. The repeated passing of the herd along the narrow path has broken through and compacted the snow, and the pellets of scat have composted into a kind of sand, giving their narrow hooves traction. As the going becomes easier, I understand how the deer can break into a run, white tails flashing, without breaking their legs. I follow the trail across the face of the ridge. It's too cold to stay out long. As I turn to retrace my steps, I pause to look from this new perspective at the window where I had sat and watched the deer and would sit and watch again.
>
> **References**
>
> Johnson, D. (2018). *What to feed wild deer*. Accessed at https://sciencing.com/feed-wild-deer-5495043.html on February 24, 2020.
>
> Wiley, J., & Hulsey, C. (n.d.). *Living on the edge: How deer survive winter*. Accessed at https://www.maine.gov/ifw/docs/deer_yards.pdf on May 21, 2020.

Figure 4.2: Narrative with research added—Deer watch.

Sources

The internet has made information on just about any topic immediately and easily available to students and, simultaneously, reduced the visibility of the authors of that information. The information just seems to be there in cyberspace, ready to use. When students are old enough to support their ideas with external sources, they are old enough to give credit to those sources and use the material they find accurately and honestly. According to education technologist Kathy Schrock (2018), teachers can expect students in grades 1 through 5 to make incremental progress each year in citing key elements of a source. For example, you can ask a first-grade student to cite author and title in a straightforward way: "I learned how caterpillars become butterflies from a book by Gail Gibbons. The title of the book is *Monarch Butterfly*." For elementary students, it's important to encourage them to use books and periodicals where authors' names are easy to find and long URLs are not an issue. Formatting can come later when sources and their use become more complex. By grade 3, a student is capable of including actual citations, adding details to author and title, including the publication date, and applying format conventions such as quotation marks and italics. By the time students reach fifth grade, they can provide all the elements of a formal citation. From sixth grade on, students will be capable of toggling back and forth between multiple citation-style systems: Modern Language Association (MLA), American Psychological Association (APA), Chicago style, and so on. This incremental progress requires teacher modeling, coaching, and persistence. But don't drive your students wild with frustration over the intricacies of citations they are simply not developmentally ready to handle.

As with all aspects of language, human beings have an immense ability to learn the rules of correct usage once those rules become important. That moment doesn't always coincide with the lesson on source citation; it comes when students reach a development level that includes consciousness of what their work says about them to others. In my experience, this is around age sixteen, which means that students may be subjected to years of worksheets and red pencil marks on their work about matters they just don't see as important. In order for following the rules to matter to students, they need to come up naturally in the writing students are doing. Trying to enforce them before students are ready can actually be harmful. In an article for *The Atlantic*, Michelle Navarre Cleary (2014), an educator and researcher, opens with this statement: "A century of research shows that traditional grammar lessons—those hours spent diagramming sentences and memorizing parts of speech—don't help and may even hinder students' efforts to become better writers." She adds that this is true across all grade levels (Cleary, 2014). Cleary (2014) describes one study that followed three groups of students from ninth to eleventh grade. One group had traditional rule-bound lessons, a second received instruction about writing rules using an alternative approach, and the third group had no lessons on rules, "just more literature and creative writing" (Cleary, 2014). The only difference at the end of the study was that the rule-bound groups "emerged with a strong antipathy to English" (Cleary, 2014).

In a student-centered classroom, it's natural to pay attention to what students already know, what they are not yet ready to learn, and when they need information about rules of writing. Students across grade levels and content areas arrive in any given classroom with their own unique experiences and background knowledge (Darling-Hammond, Flook, Cook-Harvey, Barron, & Osher, 2019). In fact, these differences can serve as a springboard:

> The fact that background knowledge is important for higher level problem solving does not mean that "basic skills" must be taught by rote before children engage in inquiry. In fact, allowing for discovery and exploration can help set the stage for explicit instruction. (Darling-Hammond et al., 2019)

Darling-Hammond et al. (2019) highlight an approach called inventing to prepare for future learning, which was advanced in 1999 by John D. Bransford and Daniel L. Schwartz. They conclude that this approach, which challenges learners and uses inquiry, means better recall and understanding of later learning than simply teaching them facts (Darling-Hammond et al., 2019). In terms, specifically, of rules about source citation, it is crucial to provide opportunities for a wide variety of writing experiences first and get to the rules when students are ready to use them in work that matters to them. You can make information about the fine points of usage available for students who are ready without penalizing those who are not.

Format

Researched narrative should have the natural flow of a well-told and convincingly detailed story. Depending on how much emphasis teachers previously placed on the five-paragraph essay, there might be some unlearning for students to do. You can't always convince students there are other ways to organize a piece of writing just by saying so. Teachers might need to demonstrate to students that good writing does not require adherence to the five-paragraph format and that, in fact, a five-paragraph essay is nearly impossible to find in the real world.

As I recall, it took me an entire class period to convince a group of sophomores that there is more than one way to structure an essay. We were in the middle of a unit focused on the culture of youth, reading and talking about cultural norms relevant to teenagers. In this context, I asked students to make a list of the groups they belonged to, including family, friends, sports, activities, classes, jobs, and so on. Then I asked them to write next to each group its unwritten rules (for example, friends don't gossip about one another and members of a baseball team need to hustle when taking the field). Next, I asked if membership in a group ever required them to follow a rule they didn't agree with. This provoked more writing and sharing, mostly about going along when friends engaged in behavior the individual privately did not condone. An example that came up several times was pressure from peers to jump off a local bridge to prove you've got the right stuff. Describing a night on this bridge looked like an engaging way to get started writing a piece. But students wanted to tack on a thesis: *resisting the call to jump takes more courage than jumping*. "That's beautiful," I said, "but you need to save it for the conclusion. Make sure the reader knows what your topic is from the get-go, but don't give your position away so early in the writing." We agreed it would be important to discuss the inner conflict, explain why it's so hard to say *no* to peers, and give equal time to why it's so important to stand on your own two feet. Throughout the essay, the choices students made about what to include would foreshadow their thesis, gradually informing and influencing the reader in preparation for a full statement of the thesis in the concluding paragraph. Then, that thesis would fully resonate with readers. There was a nice a-ha moment when students realized if they saved their thesis statement for the conclusion, they wouldn't be repeating themselves.

A pair of articles from *Education Week* suggests the wide range in thinking among educators about the form writing should take. Some teachers insist on the five-paragraph essay, and others are wary about teaching students formulas. One teacher suggests formulaic writing structures help students with learning disabilities organize their thoughts (Sawchuk, 2016). Influential literacy educator Lucy Calkins, who has long been a leader in taking a workshop approach to writing, advocates variety in writing instruction (Rebora, 2016). The bottom line is that teachers and students should not assume that the five-paragraph essay is their only choice; students can organize their narratives with much more freedom.

Calkins used to focus on personal narrative, which can take the form of both prose and poetry, but she has been working with colleagues to give students experience writing for multiple purposes: to persuade and inform as well as narrate (Rebora, 2016). When the writer's purpose is to inform, there are at least five text structures to draw on: (1) description, (2) problem–solution, (3) chronology, (4) compare–contrast, and (5) cause–effect. These alternatives to the five-paragraph format provide guidance but also freedom. The structure of a piece of writing should develop naturally to fit the writer's purpose, which might be to describe and discuss the impact of an event (description and cause–effect), to compare how two contrasting perspectives on an issue have changed over time (compare–contrast and chronology), or to provide background information and possible ways to solve a complicated problem (cause–effect and problem–solution). As you can see, each of these examples requires at least two types of text structure. Students might focus on a single structure just to practice using it, but any piece of writing that really matters to a student is likely to require more than one structure.

When the writer's purpose is to persuade, there are two approaches: (1) deduction and (2) induction. The five-paragraph format is deductive in that the writer states the thesis in the opening paragraph, supports the thesis in three body paragraphs, and restates the thesis in the conclusion. The inductive approach is a bit more subtle. It uses the opening paragraph to introduce the topic and draw the reader in. The body of the essay can have as many paragraphs as necessary to inform and influence the reader to move toward the writer's position on the topic. The conclusion reveals that position.

According to education journalist Stephen Sawchuk (2016), teacher-preparation programs might fall short of providing guidance on writing instruction, making the five-paragraph essay an easy and familiar fallback for many teachers. I recommend Purdue University's Global Writing Center at http://library.purdueglobal.edu/writingcenter as a great resource that provides definitions of text structures and approaches to argument.

Field Research

Once students feel at home with researched narratives based on their own life experiences, they can look to the larger world for material. The inspiration to open the classroom and school doors to admit field research came from Laury Fischer, who presented the notion in his Proteus Project in the summer of 1988 when I participated in the Bay Area Writing Project Summer Open Program. When we got back in touch recently, Laury described how the project began: "I developed Proteus when I was teaching second-semester high school seniors—who were accepted to college and could barely care anymore about school. Proteus seemed to motivate them" (L. Fischer, personal communication, January 2020). I launched the Proteus Project in my own classes at Newtown High School and found that it motivated a wide range of students to engage in highly original and meaningful research and writing.

When conducting *field research*, students learn about topics in an experiential manner. Elementary students can conduct field research with family and family friends. Secondary students can range further afield to support their independence, but their research should still be local and close enough to home to protect their safety. My students explored topics ranging from adoption to Zen Buddhism, from building a bridge to young love, from cancer to xenophobia—and everything in between. The possibilities are as many as there are students with the curiosity to know more about their world.

Elementary students may need support from the teacher and their peers to decide on a topic. Brainstorming as a class or using a low-risk list-making approach to generate lots of ideas helps students of all ages realize how many possible topics there are. And, these protocols also give students a chance to feel an affinity for a topic they might not have thought of themselves. Following is a typical protocol a teacher might use to facilitate student brainstorming.

1. Give students about five minutes to make a list of ten topics they know something about. Tell students to write down what comes to mind as fast as they can. No topic is too silly or too strange—just add it to the list.

2. Ask students to pick one item from the list to share, and write the shared items on the board. The only rule is that a shared item can't repeat one already on the board. Refrain from commenting on topics, just record them.

3. Give students another five minutes to make a list of topics they would like to know more about. Again, ask students to pick one item to share, and record the items on the board.

4. At this point, the board should be full of possible topics. Ask students to put a star next to the three topics that interest them most. The starred topics can be on each student's own lists, on the shared group list on the board, or both.

5. Invite students to meet in peer-conference groups (see chapter 1, page 11) to talk about their ideas and help one another decide which topics are the most interesting.

The more latitude students receive to make choices about topics, the more invested they are likely to be in both the research and academic writing, and the higher they are likely to reach toward achievement of learning goals. Figure 4.3 (page 70) and figure 4.4 (page 71) provide additional guidelines for elementary and secondary students developing a researched narrative.

Adults are generally eager to help students with field-research projects and can be incredibly generous with the time needed to be interviewed or complete a survey, and for secondary students, to arrange to visit the adoption agency, the Buddhist temple, the Brooklyn Bridge, the young adult advice columnist's office, the local hospice, or the regional National Association for the Advancement of Colored People (NAACP) branch. It's important to meet with students early in the field-research process to help them identify a compelling topic that is already part of their lives in some way. For students, field research is an opportunity to broaden and deepen their knowledge of a topic they want to know more about, not to start from scratch in a new field.

> The purpose of this checklist is to help you organize while you work on a writing project with multiple steps.
> - ☐ Choose a topic that is truly interesting to you.
> - ☐ Write a narrative based on what you already know about this topic. For example, let's say your topic is raising chickens and selling their eggs to neighbors. This might be something you do yourself or something a parent or older sibling does. You could write a narrative about your first experience with a chicken or a day in the life of a chicken rancher, or what it was like on the night a fox got into the chicken coop.
> - ☐ Gather more information from an interview and survey. Your interview could be with a family member or friend who raises chickens. You could survey your classmates to find out how much they know about raising chickens.
> - ☐ Add the information from the interview and survey to your narrative, which will make it a researched narrative.
> - ☐ Illustrate the researched narrative with photos from your interview or your own drawings about your topic.
> - ☐ Include a graph that shows your survey results.
> - ☐ Decide on a title for your researched narrative.

Figure 4.3: Researched narrative guidelines for elementary students.

*Visit **go.SolutionTree.com/instruction** for a free reproducible version of this figure.*

For some students, the heart of the story becomes their own venture into the larger world. For others, the focus narrows to an individual whose compelling experience represents that of others. And a few students look at the big picture, trying to convey what it was like to be present at an historic time and place. I remember a student who visited the local chapter of U.S. Department of Veterans Affairs and, through her interviews, began to learn about MIAs (soldiers missing in action and almost certainly dead, but whose bodies had not yet been found and returned to their families for burial and closure). My students and I were riveted as she took us along on a journey that was both tragic and inspiring.

Interviews

Students need to prepare background research and questions ahead of time to make the most of field-research interviews, surveys, and visits. Conducting a good interview requires flexibility as well as preparation. Give elementary students guidelines (see figure 4.5, page 72) and time to practice with their peers. Elementary students should limit their search for an interview subject to family members and well-known family friends. Conducting an interview, even with someone they already know, will help elementary students develop confidence in their ability to hold their own in a conversation with an adult.

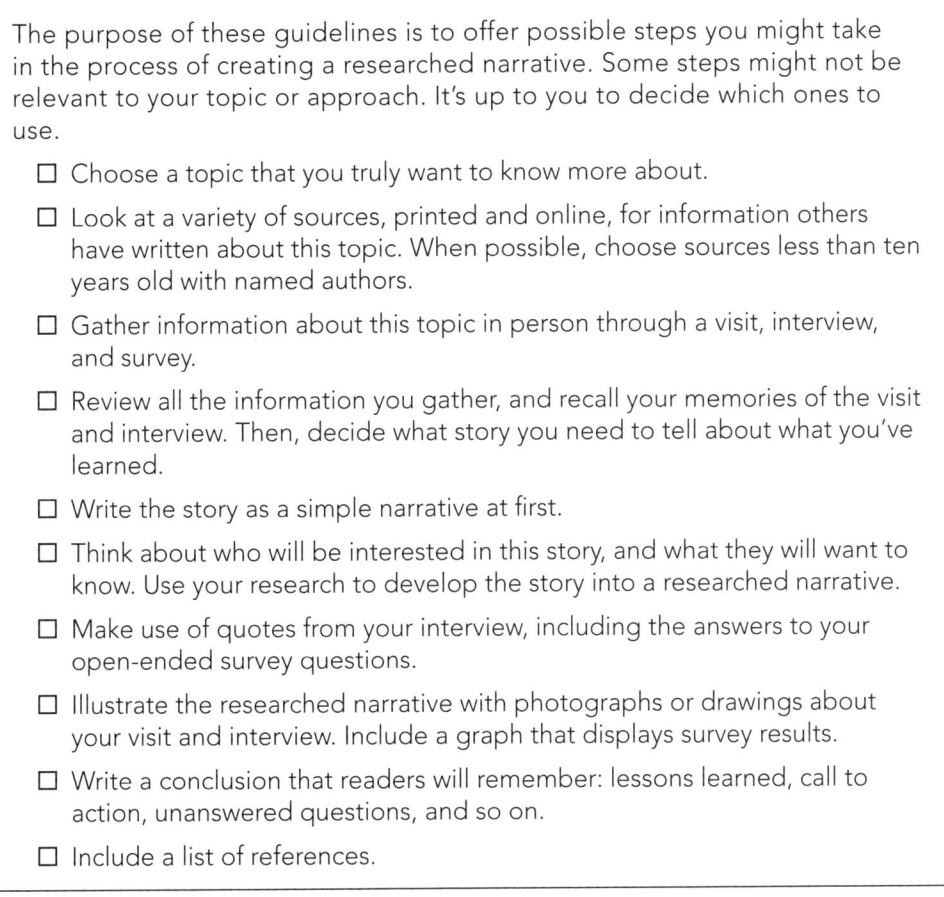

Figure 4.4: Researched narrative guidelines for secondary students.

Visit go.SolutionTree.com/instruction for a free reproducible version of this figure.

Ask secondary students to generate a list of about ten questions, starting with objective questions that are comfortable to answer and then moving gradually toward more subjective questions that might not be so comfortable to answer. Of course, students need to be wary of offending an interview subject, as that might bring the interview to a premature end. However, encourage students to let their questions express genuine curiosity and a desire to really know what there is to know about the subject. Secondary students also need time to practice and some coaching to not adhere rigidly to the prepared list if the interview subject talks readily and goes in unanticipated but interesting and helpful directions. Give secondary students guidelines (see figure 4.6, page 73) and time to practice in class. The practice sessions have the added benefit of preparing secondary students for college and job interviews in their own not-too-distant futures.

> Conducting an interview with an expert is an exciting way to learn more about a topic that interests you. To make the best use of the opportunity and to be polite to the person you're interviewing, there are some things you need to prepare ahead of time and other things you need to remember to do during the interview.
>
> - ☐ Ask the family member or family friend when would be a convenient time for the interview. It's fine to have a parent or older sibling with you for the interview.
> - ☐ Agree ahead of time about how long the interview will take. Fifteen to twenty minutes is about right.
> - ☐ Write down what you already know about the person you are interviewing. Then write down questions that will help you learn more. Let's say you are interviewing a family member or family friend who is a police officer. You could ask questions like, "Why did you become a police officer? What do you have to do to become a police officer? What's the hardest, best, strangest, or funniest thing you've had to do as a police officer? What's your advice for kids who want to become police officers?"
> - ☐ Be on time and say, "Thank you for taking time to talk to me."
> - ☐ Bring a notebook and pencil or pen.
> - ☐ If available, you could also bring a smart phone (or other devices) that can take photos, videos, and record sound. Be sure to say, "May I take a photo?" before you do so.
> - ☐ When your time is up, say, "Thank you for helping me learn more about your work."
> - ☐ Add what you learned from the interview to the writing you have already done.

Figure 4.5: Interview guidelines for elementary students.

*Visit **go.SolutionTree.com/instruction** for a free reproducible version of this figure.*

Even though technology makes it possible to conduct an interview via email or other means, I encouraged my students to meet face-to-face with their interview subjects so they could describe a specific place and time, and also gather telling details about the interview subject's manner of speaking, appearance, and so on. These skills require students to set up, conduct, and follow up on an interview, all important to the quality of the writing the student will eventually do about the interview.

Surveys

Conducting a survey makes it possible for students to get a more wide-reaching perspective on their topic. Survey questions can be similar to interview questions, except more of them must be in a quantifiable format (that is, *yes* or *no*, true or false, or multiple choice). Instead of going on a deep dive with one or a few people in

> Conducting an interview with an expert is an exciting way to learn more about a topic that interests you. To make the best use of the opportunity and to be polite to the person you're interviewing, there are quite a few things you need to do before, during, and after the interview. The purpose of this checklist is to help you do a good job of managing the interview process.
>
> ☐ Set up an appointment at a time and place that is convenient to the interview subject, and be specific about how long the interview will last (half an hour to an hour).
>
> ☐ Prepare questions ahead of time.
>
> ☐ Gather materials, including a notebook, writing utensil, recording device, and camera.
>
> ☐ Be on time for the appointment.
>
> ☐ Express gratitude for the time the interview subject is giving to the project.
>
> ☐ Ask the interview subject's permission to record the interview and take a photo or shoot video.
>
> ☐ Stay within the agreed-on time limit.
>
> ☐ Review notes and recordings promptly to determine whether or not you need to ask follow-up questions.
>
> ☐ Thank the interview subject in person at the end of the interview, and send a note or email with further thanks and any follow-up questions.
>
> ☐ Quote the interview subject accurately and in context.
>
> ☐ Include the interview subject's name in the list of references.

Figure 4.6: Interview guidelines for secondary students.

*Visit **go.SolutionTree.com/instruction** for a free reproducible version of this figure.*

interviews, they can get opinions from many more people. They might discover that others do not share their opinions. Conducting a survey as a class will help elementary students practice applying their mathematics skills to an interesting topic. With practice, elementary students can design and conduct a survey on their own with guidelines (figure 4.7, page 74) to remind them of the steps.

Secondary students can design and conduct a survey with guidelines from the teacher and some peer feedback. Challenge secondary students to consider the nuances of writing effective survey questions. Students must be aware of their own biases and take care not to write *leading questions* (questions that direct survey respondents to predetermined answers). You can also introduce secondary students to the idea of including multiple items about the same question. Let's say the overall topic is civil rights. If there are three different questions about voting rights instead of just one, the results are more likely to be accurate and significant.

> The purpose of this checklist is to help you create, conduct, and use survey results.
>
> ☐ Write five or more questions the survey respondent can answer with *yes* or *no*.
>
> ☐ Write one question the survey respondent can answer with one or two sentences.
>
> ☐ Ask a classmate to help you revise each question so it is easier to understand. If the questions are unclear, the survey results will be inaccurate.
>
> ☐ Ask all the people in a group to complete the survey. The group might consist of all the members of your class, all the members of an after-school activity, all the teachers in your school, and so on.
>
> ☐ Use your mathematics skills to convert the *yes* or *no* answers into percentages. You need to know what percentage of survey respondents answered *yes* and what percentage answered *no* for each question.
>
> ☐ Make a graph that shows the survey results.

Figure 4.7: Survey guidelines for elementary students.

*Visit **go.SolutionTree.com/instruction** for a free reproducible version of this figure.*

Students can represent survey results in various kinds of graphs to give the project a visual element. A final more open-ended question can provide insights and quotable material, but the primary goal of the survey is to gather data from a statistically significant percentage of a target population. For relatively small surveys intended to get a rough idea of what people think about a topic, data scientist Piroska Bisits Bullen (2013) recommends aiming for 10 percent of the target population in order to generate meaningful data. For populations of less than one hundred, such as the students in one classroom, one should generally try to survey everyone in the population (Bullen, 2013). My students often identified their graduating class as the target population. If there were four hundred students in the class, then forty of them need to complete the survey for the data to be significant. However, online tools such as SurveyMonkey (www.surveymonkey.com) make it possible for students to survey a target population they don't have day-to-day contact with. Figure 4.8 offers students a worksheet to stay organized while they're working on the survey.

Ask students to get feedback on their surveys (figure 4.9, page 76) before printing or posting them online. It can take a lot of revision before survey questions are concise and clear enough to produce reliable results.

Use to stay organized	Reflect on how the survey went
Designing, conducting, and analyzing survey results are useful skills in a wide range of subject areas and situations. If this is your first formal survey, it probably won't be your last! Use the following worksheet to stay organized while you're working on the survey and to reflect on how it went when the survey is complete. What did you do? How did it go? What would you change? Reflecting on these questions will help your next survey be even better.	
Write at least ten questions in a quantifiable format (*yes* or *no*, true or false, multiple choice).	
Include one or two open-ended questions.	
Get peer feedback on your questions before you make copies of the survey or post it online. It can take a lot of revisions before survey questions are concise and clear enough to produce reliable results.	
Conduct the survey with at least 10 percent of your target population if it is more than one hundred.	
Convert the quantifiable responses into a graph.	
Use responses to open-ended questions to support your discussion of the survey and your researched narrative as a whole.	

Figure 4.8: Survey guidelines for secondary students.

*Visit **go.SolutionTree.com/instruction** for a free reproducible version of this figure.*

Narrative Devices

Field research with primary sources helps students experience the thrill both journalists and novelists feel when they sense a good story that needs to be told and immerse themselves in people, places, and events, so they can get at the human truth of the story and tell it with both authority and art. Once they've done the research, it's time to write about it. To help students write a story well, I found that they benefit from being aware of four narrative devices fiction writers, researchers, and nonfiction writers employ to engage readers, which Tom Wolfe (1973) describes in his seminal work *The New Journalism*.

Use this worksheet to provide feedback about other students' survey questions.	
Questions	**Comments and suggestions**
Subject: Is the subject too broad or too narrow? Offer suggestions for a sharper focus.	
Target population: Is the target population appropriate to the subject? How large is this population? Is it feasible to survey all of it (if it's less than one hundred) or at least 10 percent if it's one hundred or more?	
Survey items: Given what you know of the writer's expectations, do the questions reveal bias? Do the questions tend to lead the survey respondent in a certain direction? Suggest one or more additional questions.	
Question format: Has the writer provided about ten questions? Are most of the questions quantifiable (*yes* or *no*, true or false, multiple choice, and so on)? Suggest an alternative format for one or more questions.	
Survey format: Has the writer included his or her name, survey purpose, a survey title, clear directions, and a thank-you? If not, suggest what the writer needs to add.	
Feedback from _____	

Figure 4.9: Survey-feedback guidelines for secondary students.

Visit **go.SolutionTree.com/instruction** *for a free reproducible version of this figure.*

1. **Scene-by-scene construction:** The writer knows everything that happened between points A and Z in a series of events, but including everything bogs down the story. The writer must make hard decisions about what will move the core narrative forward and what can and should be left out.

2. **Realistic dialogue:** The writer who can record and recreate authentic dialogue (and monologue) has the power to make the reader feel present at the scene. What people say, how they say it, and what people don't say tell the reader so much about them.

3. **Status life details:** The term *status life* refers to a kind of detail that conveys information indirectly to the reader about who people are (or think they are). For example, you can ask your students to notice the various ways people dress, how they occupy a chair, and the gear they carry. These details suggest a great deal about their personal history and attitude toward life.

4. **Point of view:** Writing in first person (I) gives the work immediacy and intimacy. Third person (they) provides flexibility for the writer to describe events that he or she could not have witnessed in person. Both approaches have merits. The writer needs to decide which works best for the work at hand.

The summaries of the four devices offered here are not for the purpose of teaching students to use them but, instead, to help teachers be aware of them. They can be a resource when teachers have conversations with students about their researched narrative writing. I've found that students will benefit when their teacher can suggest taking a different point of view, notice an interesting detail, or point out a lively exchange of dialogue. And, most important, students need to hear their teacher say, "Don't try to cover everything that happened in your story. You're the writer. You get to decide what's important and what can be left out."

Once students complete their researched narratives, they will relish an opportunity to present their work to the class or participate in a read-and-respond session. Ask students to put their researched narratives in a binder with a pocket or simply clip the pages together with an envelope. Then ask everyone to place their projects on a table in the center of the room. Invite students to pick someone else's researched narrative to read and respond to with a note about what they liked. Students then tuck the notes in the binder pocket or the clipped-on envelope. When students have had time to read and respond to about five projects, it's time to close the session. Ask each student to retrieve his or her own researched narrative, and then give all students some time to enjoy the notes about their work from their classmates.

Secondary students enjoy a read-and-respond session as much as elementary students. Consider inviting students to post their researched narratives to a blog you monitor. Whether elementary or secondary, when students have experienced writing narratives with researched primary sources about topics that matter to them, the strategies that make writing and research exciting are theirs to keep. The likelihood grows that they will, first of all, find interesting ways to approach more typical academic-writing assignments and, even more important, they will come to see writing as an enjoyable aspect of a full life.

Letters to the Editor

Reading and writing letters to the editor invites students to get acquainted with what people have to say about contemporary issues and, of course, to weigh in. Classrooms in the United States are fortunate to have access to a free press and a wide range of national and local newspapers. It's interesting to read what experienced commentators have to say about the issues of the day, and it can be especially exciting to hear from friends and neighbors. I admit to turning first to the editorial (op-ed) and letters pages of the newspaper. *Letters to the editor* (LTEs) are short, deal with contemporary topics, and have the potential for publication in the larger world, as well as in the classroom.

As students read and discuss LTEs together, ask them to be on the lookout for a writer whose style and ideas resonate with them to use as a source of inspiration. Once students are acquainted with the format, you can give them the guidelines in figure 4.10 or figure 4.11 and invite them to research and write an original LTE.

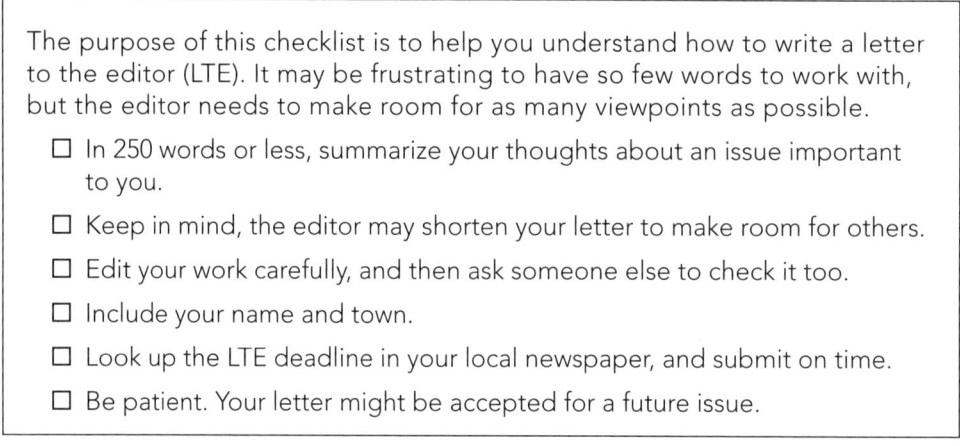

The purpose of this checklist is to help you understand how to write a letter to the editor (LTE). It may be frustrating to have so few words to work with, but the editor needs to make room for as many viewpoints as possible.

- ☐ In 250 words or less, summarize your thoughts about an issue important to you.
- ☐ Keep in mind, the editor may shorten your letter to make room for others.
- ☐ Edit your work carefully, and then ask someone else to check it too.
- ☐ Include your name and town.
- ☐ Look up the LTE deadline in your local newspaper, and submit on time.
- ☐ Be patient. Your letter might be accepted for a future issue.

Figure 4.10: Letter to the editor guidelines for elementary students.

*Visit **go.SolutionTree.com/instruction** for a free reproducible version of this figure.*

LTEs summon students to look beyond the classroom for their audience and provide an intriguing opportunity for students to demonstrate their progress toward achievement of researched-writing learning goals.

The requirements for submitting a LTE are usually simple and user friendly. Some publications prefer to receive student work in a batch, with a cover letter from the teacher. The editor may publish a few of the students' letters in the regular LTE column or use them in a feature story about what's going on in the schools.

Stay organized	Reflect on your progress
\multicolumn{2}{l}{The letter to the editor (LTE) provides an opportunity to demonstrate your ability to use important skills: conducting research, developing a position on an issue, demonstrating awareness of the audience, and reflecting on your work. Use this worksheet to stay organized and reflect on how you're doing. Where do you see growth? What changes have you made? What still needs work?}	

Stay organized	Reflect on your progress
Research	
Read several LTEs to become familiar with the format and requirements. Select a current issue that is important to you, and find out what other people think by searching reliable online or print sources. You will need to cite one or two experts in your LTE about the issue.	
Develop a position	
Use the writing process to deepen your understanding of the issue (draft, get feedback, rethink, draft some more, get more feedback, revise again). When you can articulate and support a clear position on the issue, you are ready for fine-tuning.	
Demonstrate awareness of your audience	
Think about the editor who will decide whether to publish your LTE. You want this very important person to think your LTE is informative and lively, original, and appropriate. Fine-tune your work to achieve a style that suits you and is suitable for a LTE. The editor will expect your LTE to be free of usage errors. Proofread carefully, and then ask group members to check your work.	
In consultation with your teacher, submit your LTE to a local newspaper for publication, adhering to the guidelines in the newspaper.	

Figure 4.11: Letter to the editor guidelines for secondary students.

Visit go.SolutionTree.com/instruction for a free reproducible version of this figure.

With writing, the aim is to give each student many ways to reach as many people as possible while making the task engaging and rewarding. Now we'll move on to reading, where the aim is to soak up as many perspectives as possible, with the same goal.

Illumination of the Process of Reading

Reading opens doors to so many aspects of daily life: the newspaper, legal documents, signage, and letters from friends and family members. And, of course, books also open doors to history, mathematics, science, and the imaginative work of poets, playwrights, and novelists. Some people teach themselves to read, but most learn to read in school, building word recognition and comprehension strategies with time and practice. At some point—and it is certainly not the same point for everyone—reading is like riding a bike. You just do it. Until then, students need a wide range of positive reading experiences to gradually build their skills and confidence. Over time, the process of reading becomes invisible, going on in our minds with little outward indication. Speaking and writing are visible. Even listening can be visible if the listener uses body language to indicate attention, agreement, surprise, and so on. But reading is largely invisible and can seem inaccessible to the uninitiated.

In turn, unveiling the processes of reading is a powerful way to improve achievement. In 2013 when Alexa Sorden became the new principal of a failing elementary school in a high-poverty Bronx neighborhood, she decided that literacy was the key to her students' success across subject areas (Berwick, 2019). Sorden developed a collaborative approach to reading that combines choral reading with close reading. This approach breaks the task of reading into manageable chunks and calls on students to work together to decode, comprehend, and, ultimately, appreciate and enjoy challenging texts. This collaborative approach to reading has resulted in dramatic increases in student achievement in all subject areas, as well as successful transitions from elementary to secondary school (Berwick, 2019). Kianna Beato, a graduate and current seventh grader, says, "I was prepared because the teachers taught me well . . . I knew there was nothing to be afraid of in a different school" (as cited in Berwick, 2019).

The collaborative approach to reading developed by Sorden is similar to the approach I experienced in workshops designed for teachers at Bard College's Institute for Writing and Thinking. This workshop approach called on teachers to collaborate with one another in the process of gradually getting acquainted with challenging texts. When students are engaged in collaboration with other students in a flexible workshop setting, teachers have the time and opportunity to meet with individuals and small groups, learn about students' strengths and needs, and plan around their interests. It's typical for a reading workshop to include a minilesson or two about some aspect of reading that is currently important to students, time for students to read and confer with one another, and time to come together as a class to share (Kittle, n.d.; Units of Study, n.d.). The approach I've taken combines the collaborative approach described by education journalist Carly Berwick (2019) with the flexibility of a reading workshop.

Text-based discussions are a bit more formal than a collaborative reading workshop, but students who are ready to talk about what they're reading benefit from this type of experience. The teacher provides the framework for a text-based discussion, but students run the show. In the following sections you will find information about setting up collaborative reading workshops and text-based discussions, both of which give students opportunities to deepen their understanding of texts and to increase their appreciation for how much readers can accomplish when they work together. Both collaborative reading workshops and text-based discussions can help make reading visible. These approaches are beneficial for all readers, in part, because they create the circumstances in which less-experienced readers encountering a challenging text can learn from more sophisticated readers.

Collaborative Reading Workshop

Students need opportunities to develop confidence in their individual responses to issues, ideas, and texts, and to experience the evolution of thinking that happens when they share their responses with peers and teachers. A *collaborative reading workshop* provides teacher-guided practice with the reading skills often invisible to students. These strategies make what experienced readers do explicit. Talking through a text aloud automatically slows the process, so there is time for students to think about and grasp details and nuances. Once the teacher models this process, students can use the same approach in collaborative groups, building confidence through practicing their ability to handle course material, directions and questions on standardized tests, and other reading challenges they will encounter in school and in their lives beyond.

A workshop approach to reading is *recursive*, toggling back and forth between reception and expression to generate, develop, and articulate thoughts on the text at hand. Collaborative reading workshops need to provide space for private and shared writing, and, like many student-centered strategies, the teacher should invite response without directing it to a predetermined path. The goal is for participants to think independently, not to discover what you have in mind. The amount of text should be small. Elementary students could tackle a single poem or short story. Secondary students might look at an essay rather than an entire book, a chapter rather than a novel, or six poems instead of a complete collection. Collaborative reading workshops are not limited to traditional written text. When *text* is more broadly interpreted to include anything that can be observed and interpreted, the focus of a workshop can be on a work of art, a sign or cultural icon, a photo, or a film clip. Limiting the amount of material to consider is an important step when students are building reading skills. What follows are seven techniques teachers can use to get students thinking, writing, and talking about reading.

1. Note to self
2. Shift in perspective
3. Response to prompts
4. Bumper sticker
5. Background information
6. Break it down
7. Quaker read

A collaborative reading workshop with elementary students should focus on just one or two of these techniques, while secondary students could handle several in a single workshop. They work on a wide range of materials, but they are especially helpful when students are tackling a challenging text. The techniques help students slow down, pay close attention, and think hard. I'll discuss each in further detail in the following sections.

Note to Self

Giving students a little time to write whatever happens to be on their minds, along with assurances that you will not ask them to share what they write, is the equivalent of warming up before a run or taking a deep breath before walking into a meeting. Try providing five minutes of writing time for the purpose of clearing the mind in preparation for close and collaborative work with challenging material.

Shift in Perspective

A shift in perspective gives students a chance to become acquainted with the material with no need just yet to decide what it means. Try playing with the material in ways that encourage students to see it from a new perspective: turn an image upside down, alternate reading lines of a text between two voices from opposite sides of the room, play a film clip backward, read a passage from a text slowly in unison, and so on.

Response to Prompts

The first part of the prompt is to pose a question that everyone will have something to say about. For example, think about the different roles you play in a single day—scholar, athlete, artist, friend, family member, significant other, and so on. How do these roles define who you are?

The second part of the prompt is to apply the question to the material under consideration. For example, when elementary students are looking at American painter and illustrator Norman Rockwell's (1964) painting, *The Problem We All Live With*, which shows Ruby Bridges walking to Frantz Elementary School flanked by four U.S. marshals, they could guess what it was like for her to try to learn in that previously all-White school. They could imagine what it would be like to be her sibling or her friend. When secondary students are looking at a combination of poems by Walt

Whitman such as "I Hear America Singing," "I Hear It Was Charged Against Me," "Beat! Beat! Drums!" and examples of his memorandums from Civil War field hospitals (Whitman, 1995), it would be possible for them to guess the roles Whitman saw himself playing and how these roles defined him.

Once students have had time to write responses to both parts of the prompt, invite them to share in small groups. It's important to emphasize that students need to read what they actually wrote rather than summarize it. The risk is a little greater in reading the actual written words, but the language tends to be richer and more precise than talking about what you wrote.

Bumper Sticker

The process of condensing something to its essence—whether it takes the form of a bumper sticker or an elevator speech—can be fun and also call on students to do some serious thinking.

Invite students to select words and phrases from their response to prompts to create a short slogan that could fit on a bumper sticker, a poem, or a caption for a drawing that captures the essence of their response. Invite students to share these creations in small groups.

Background Information

Some say you should interpret a text as a stand-alone (without background information), while others say background information is vital to full understanding. It's important to take both approaches.

Provide some additional information about the material under consideration, which could be a biographical note, like something going on in political or social history that might have influenced the material and its author. Encourage students to make notes about this information, including questions that have begun to occur to them.

Break It Down

Solving a problem by breaking it down into several smaller problems is a time-honored strategy and works with reading too. Tackle a longer section of the text or a complex image in small chunks, such as a stanza of a poem or a paragraph of prose or an area within an image, literally covering up the rest of the text to focus on the single stanza or paragraph or area. Have each student record ideas about each chunk and then discuss the process and findings with a partner. For elementary students, display each chunk on a screen, and record their findings together as a class.

Quaker Read

Quaker read is a way to share individual responses without the teacher having to call on each student. This technique makes it possible to quickly sample the responses of an entire class. The cumulative impact of Quaker read is considerable, giving the teacher a quick glimpse into each student's evolving response to the material and giving everyone a sense of the whole class's response.

Once students have had a chance to think and rethink about the material and what it says to them, ask each student to select a line, sentence, or detail that seems to be especially significant and write about whatever the selection suggests. When the text under consideration is a visual image, ask students to focus on an area or element they find significant and write about it. Then invite all members of the class to share at least one line from their response in Quaker read style, without the teacher calling on them. At this point, teachers can certainly ask students to develop and organize their ideas into a response, but, in terms of actual learning, most of the work has already been done. All that may be necessary is an opportunity for students to write a final reflective comment.

Once the format and techniques of collaborative reading workshops are familiar to students, you can give students the opportunity to serve as facilitators, choosing the material and guiding their peers through the collaborative reading process. The use of collaborative reading workshop techniques prepares students to participate fully in text-based discussions.

Text-Based Discussions

Once students experience working slowly through a text, building and affirming their individual response in collaboration with classmates, they are ready for a more formal text-based discussion. While a lively discussion can include an entire class, it's just about impossible to attain the depth and detail of a good text-based discussion with so many participants. Dividing the class into two or three groups makes it possible to include many and varied perspectives and still maintain a sufficient sense of intimacy for quieter group members to feel comfortable participating. Students or the teacher can determine group members, or the teacher can draw groups randomly. Over time, the important thing is for everyone in the class to have a chance to work with everyone else.

For *text-based discussions*, I adapted education consultant and coach Gene Thompson-Grove's (n.d.) guidelines, available through the National School Reform Faculty. The guidelines in figure 4.12 and figure 4.13 (page 86) emphasize the goal of the discussion—to have a natural conversation, or the kind of conversation that could occur around the dinner table or over a cup of coffee after a movie. The purpose of the discussion is to work together to deepen understanding of an issue or question, not to achieve some particular understanding. This discussion is truly student centered rather than teacher directed.

This checklist has two purposes. The first is to help you understand how to participate in a text-based discussion. The second is to help you celebrate your strengths and figure out what needs work. For each item in the Guidelines column, check the middle column when you have read the item and understand it. Check the far-right column for each item you did during the text-based discussion.		
Guidelines	**I have read and understand the item**	**I did this during the text-based discussion**
Listen actively.		
Build on what others say.		
Don't interrupt, even when you're excited about sharing an idea.		
Let the conversation flow as much as possible without raising your hand. It's OK if there are pauses or even silences.		
Avoid repeating an idea someone else has already said.		
Encourage others to share and explain their ideas.		

Source: Adapted from Thompson-Grove, n.d.

Figure 4.12: Text-based discussion guidelines for elementary students.

*Visit **go.SolutionTree.com/instruction** for a free reproducible version of this figure.*

For students to realize their full potential, discussions must be concept driven, just like any other student-centered lesson design. Students need to understand that it is their ideas that matter, not how many details from a text they can recite in the allotted time. I didn't record how many times my students spoke or penalize a student who appeared engaged but didn't speak. Some students are rapid processors, some need time to synthesize, some enjoy the sound of their own voices, and some like time to ponder the thoughts of others. Only from the combination of observation during a discussion and speaking with a student or reading a reflective comment after a discussion can the teacher gain a full understanding of what was going on in the student's mind and how high (or low) the quality of the discussion experience was from that student's perspective.

A good text-based discussion can be an intense experience as you try to balance your own active participation with encouraging and making space for others. The ability to engage in a lively and productive discussion with a group is a useful skill with a wide range of subjects and situations. Use this worksheet to get familiar with the guidelines and to reflect on how the discussion went. What did you do? How did it go? What would you change? Reflecting on these questions will help your next discussion be even better.

Get familiar with the guidelines	Reflect on your participation
Listen actively.	
Build on what others say.	
Don't interrupt, even when you're excited about sharing an idea.	
Let the conversation flow as much as possible without raising your hand. It's OK if there are pauses or even silences.	
Avoid repeating an idea someone else has already said.	
Encourage others to share and explain their ideas.	
Converse directly—there is no need to go through the facilitator.	
Be aware of and honest about your assumptions.	
Clarify, amplify, and consider the implications of your ideas and those of others.	
Support your ideas with specific references (like texts, events, and facts) and expect others to do the same.	

Source: Adapted from Thompson-Grove, n.d.

Figure 4.13: Text-based discussion guidelines for secondary students.

Visit **go.SolutionTree.com/instruction** *for a free reproducible version of this figure.*

My students took turns serving as text-based discussion facilitators. Two students can work together to fulfill this role, sharing the responsibility of keeping the group focused and moving forward. The role of facilitator rotates so that, over time, all students experience a discussion from this perspective. Lightly structured discussions give students the opportunity to realize the value of a detailed conversation to deepen ideas. The solo student, no matter how insightful, cannot develop an understanding as deep as one that results from trying out ideas, listening to the ideas of others, sharing and revisiting passages from relevant sources, and actively constructing meaning with group support. Of course, students must take responsibility for coming to discussions prepared to make meaningful contributions. Keeping the groups relatively small helps students find the courage to acknowledge their own misunderstandings and to challenge ideas not anchored in fact. The teacher's role is to monitor and provide feedback that helps students develop key skills. Sometimes a private conversation is necessary to help a student who tends to dominate the discussion understand how important it is that everyone has a chance to participate. In this situation, the teacher can ask the student to take on the challenge of helping less eager participants articulate and develop their ideas.

In the next chapter, we'll move on to the fifth student-centered teaching practice: meet individual needs in the evaluation process. I explain how to work with students as partners in the process of adapting tasks to suit strengths and needs, while helping them grow with effective feedback.

Next Steps for Deepening Understanding With Writing and Reading

The following tool details some steps you can take to deepen students' understanding with writing and reading in your classroom. For each step, note the date you tried it and reflect on how it went: What did you do? How did it go? What would you change? What's next? There are spaces available at the end for you to plan additional steps you can take toward a student-centered approach to teaching.

Next Steps Tried	Date Tried	Reflection
Select a topic, and write a short narrative about it. Do a little research, and add some factual details to your narrative. Maintain a list of references.		
Review the four devices of *The New Journalism* (Wolfe, 1973), and use them to revise and, perhaps, expand your researched narrative.		
Take a moment to try to imagine your researched narrative as a five-paragraph essay.		
Join a book club that will give you opportunities to talk about what you are reading.		

CHAPTER 5

Meet Individual Needs in the Evaluation Process

Although it didn't seem like it at the time, I got lucky early in my teaching career when a student named Aisha demanded an explanation for her marking-period grade from me. At the time, I was using a traditional system of grading; I had given her a C, but she was certain her performance deserved an A. I offered to show her the numbers in my gradebook, but she wasn't questioning my math. She was questioning my perception and my commitment to being her teacher. Aisha was not just a responsible student but also inspiring. Class activities went well because of her energy and focus. She gave much to the class, and I returned little to her, grading her work conscientiously but accepting the verdict of the numbers: her written work made Aisha a C student. Aisha moved on to her senior year, graduation, and, I hope, a life in which others recognize and generously reward her capacity for insight and skill with spoken language. She left behind a rare gift: the uneasy feeling that, even though I was sure I had done nothing wrong, *I should have done better*. This is the root of the fifth student-centered teaching practice: meeting individual needs in the evaluation process.

Before diving into how the student-centered approach works for evaluation, I want to spend a little time on traditional grading systems and the issues that come with them.

The Problems With Traditional Grading Systems

Aisha's gift spurred me to try to become a better teacher. I read books and articles and participated in workshops and conferences. Traditional grading practices can leave a student like Aisha feeling betrayed. What about Angela, whose mother had to beg her teachers to ease up on homework because her daughter wasn't getting any sleep? What about Barney, who did his homework on the fly because at home he needed to take care of a father stricken with muscular dystrophy? What about Corinne, who was so ready to move on she was cramming four years of high school into three? What about Daniel, who made one of those incredible midyear leaps but barely passed the course because of his poor first-semester performance? And what about Frank, who took a zero rather than write yet another research paper adhering to a long list of criteria?

As my concern about the impact on students of traditional grading increased, I had an opportunity to survey juniors at Newtown High School about how they define success. I sorted the responses by gender and academic level and found that every single group defined success primarily as getting the grades necessary for admission to college. Responses to two open-ended questions frequently mentioned pressure and stress related to grades. The students' comments revealed that many experienced the academic load as something to be endured in order to get into college, get a good-paying job, and, finally, sometime in the hazy future, get the security and happiness to make it all worthwhile. Teenagers are not generally recognized for their ability to delay gratification, but the survey results made it clear that delayed gratification was the norm for many teenagers, and that they carried the heavy academic load because they were afraid not to. It's just as difficult to be the student who gives up on the system as it is to be the one dutifully reading the assigned chapter and making the required notes late into the night. Either way, the pressure mounts and the stress is hard to bear.

A study from the Society for Research in Child Development (SRCD; Lee, Jamieson, Miu, Josephs, & Yeager, 2018) focuses on stress levels in ninth-grade students who are making the transition to high school. Students tend to experience a drop in grades during the first semester of high school with commensurate increase in stress. The study looked at levels of the stress hormone cortisol, which spikes in response to stress, and at daily surveys completed by students. What the researchers found was that while 68 percent of students experienced high stress in response to low grades, stress levels tended to fall after a day or two (Lee et al., 2018). However, some students' stress responses remained high much longer. There are problems with averaged grades for all students; for more vulnerable students, grade-induced stress responses can become toxic.

Harvard's National Scientific Council on the Developing Child (2014) backs this up and shows that although the human body's response to stress can be positive, in the form of increased attention and memory, sustained stress can damage a child's brain development. The report concludes:

> The future of any society depends on its ability to foster healthy development of the next generation. Extensive research on the biology of stress now shows that healthy development can be derailed by excessive or prolonged activation of stress response systems in the body and the brain, with damaging effects on learning, behavior, and health across the lifespan. (National Scientific Council on the Developing Child, 2014)

I wish I could say school-related stress is unique to secondary students, but the Harvard findings make it clear that elementary students are not exempt from feelings of pressure and anxiety. If anything, as the Harvard study points out, we need to be even more careful with elementary students because damage from stress can become a major obstacle to making progress in school and beyond (National Scientific Council on the Developing Child, 2014).

In 2008, Newtown High School, where I had taught since the early 1990s, welcomed a new principal. Dr. Charles Dumais, or Chip as he was known then, has since moved on to serve as a district superintendent, and his current position is executive director of Cooperative Educational Services, serving all the school districts in Fairfield County, Connecticut. Chip was interested in the impact of the grading system on student achievement, and thus, some faculty meetings focused on alternatives to averaged grades. At one faculty meeting, Chip distributed slips of paper with a list of ten individual grades: C, C, MA (missing assignment), D, C, B, MA, MA, B, A. He asked faculty members to assume a student had earned these grades during a marking period and invited us to determine the final grade the student should receive. The results ranged from A to F. Chip told us that researcher Douglas B. Reeves had conducted this experiment with teachers and administrators from all over the United States, with results identical to those at our faculty meeting. I was fascinated with this evidence of the disparity in grades that can result from traditional grading practices and tracked down the 2008 article in which Reeves reported his results. In his discussion of the results, Reeves (2008) writes:

> As this experiment demonstrates, the difference between failure and the honor roll often depends on the grading policies of the teacher. To reduce the failure rate, schools don't need a new curriculum, a new principal, new teachers, or new technology. They just need a better grading system.

In the 2008 article, Reeves identifies five problems with the practice of averaged grades. First, a low score, which may be more of a rebuke to the student than a reflection of his or her work quality, can do disproportionate damage to a student's marking-period average. So students who want good grades have to do whatever is necessary to receive a high grade on each and every assignment.

The second problem arises from teachers grading all assignments, thus giving formative and summative work equal impact on the final grade. If all goes well, grades on work that students do later in the marking period provide a more accurate reflection of student achievement than the average of all their earned grades. Reeves (2008) notes, "Interestingly, when teachers and administrators have been students in my graduate courses, they routinely insist that they should be evaluated on the basis of their understanding at the end of the semester rather than their work throughout the term."

Third on the list of problems is the *semester killer*, which refers to a major project late in the course that diminishes the value of the rest of the students' work and makes it difficult to know how well or poorly the student is actually doing in the course and how the student might do in the future. Fourth, teachers can use grades to punish students for not doing what they are told. Reeves (2008) cites a ninety-year compilation of evidence from grading and assessment expert Thomas R. Guskey as support for his point: punishment does not improve student performance.

And, finally, teachers talk about "my" gradebook and "giving" students grades, but the problem is larger than who owns the grades. The real question is whether or not teachers should devise their own grading system when a researcher (like Reeves) can cite such overwhelming evidence of the damage the system most high school teachers use inflicts. The practice of averaging grades to report student achievement bumps up the failure rate to the great and lasting detriment of students, the economy, and the quality of the school climate (Reeves, 2008). But the cost of failure is not only lost income and higher rates of incarceration. When the grading system sets up students to fail because of missing homework or a poor grade on a single major assignment, regardless of what the student has actually learned, the school climate suffers. On the other hand, Reeves (2008) points out, "When grading policies improve, discipline and morale almost always follow."

Nearly ten years later, in 2017, Reeves returns to the topic with an article called "Busting Myths About Grading" in which he, again, presents the problems with traditional grades, this time as five myths about grades, and discusses why these myths are so persistent. Each myth hearkens back to one of the five problems Reeves (2008) identifies in the earlier article. The five myths follow (Reeves, 2017).

- **Myth 1:** Grades motivate students.
- **Myth 2:** Grading homework and practice improves student achievement.
- **Myth 3:** Grades predict future performance.
- **Myth 4:** Punishment deters unwanted behavior.
- **Myth 5:** Grading is a personal preference.

The myths persist because it's human nature to justify what we are accustomed to doing rather than asking the hard questions about whether or not what we're doing is actually working. Reeves (2017) tells a version of the myth of Sisyphus, doomed to push a huge rock uphill for eternity, in which he stops one day to sit down on the rock and think. Reeves (2017) contends that traditional grades are a rock that teachers need to stop pushing uphill. In order for this to happen, teachers need to let go of long-held beliefs about grades, for example, "I believe that grading as punishment is effective," and replace them with hypotheses: "If I penalize students for late, incomplete, and absent homework, then student achievement will improve." Framed in this way, it's a little easier to take an objective look at the evidence, in the form of student homework completion, and determine whether or not the evidence supports the hypothesis. Reeves (2017) concludes, much as he did in the earlier article, "When we explode grading myths and establish constructive policies, the results are immediate. Reductions in failures, improvements in discipline, high levels of student engagement, and dramatic gains in teacher morale can be obtained in months, not years." As Reeves' work over the years makes clear, the problems with averaged grades haven't been resolved because teachers are still using traditional grading practices.

In my desire to be objective and adhere to the traditional grading system, I had added up and averaged grades on a whole bunch of assignments, like all teachers did. To be fair to the students who did the work, I penalized students for any assignment they turned in late or failed to complete. I once thought students who cared about getting good grades—and that would be most of them—had to put in the work necessary to earn high grades on every assignment, from the beginning to end of each marking period. But I began to realize that it took just one or two low grades (or a dreaded zero) to bring that high average tumbling down. Students had to figure out exactly what I wanted in order to earn the reward of a high grade and then produce exactly that. There was little latitude for students to try something new, take a risk, or express an individual perspective. With the best intentions in the world, I had locked my students and myself into a grading system that made compliance the first priority, creating stress and hindering their ability to learn.

And what if the teacher makes an error while entering, adding up, or averaging all assignment grades to determine the final grade? I remember a parent who asked to meet with me because she wanted to discuss her son's final grade in a certain teacher's class. I had assumed she would try to convince me, as the department head, to override the teacher's grade, and I had rehearsed my intended reply. At first my assumption seemed correct, but when I looked at the numbers, I realized they didn't add up. The parent and I put our heads together and found that, instead of the final grade in the low 80s on his report card, the student had earned a grade in the high 80s. Fortunately, our meeting ended on a pleasant note, but if this parent had not questioned the grade, it would have remained in the student's record, potentially influencing college admissions and who knows what future options. I couldn't help but wonder if I might have made such a mistake myself, but no one had caught it.

I had quieted my doubts about averaging grades by convincing myself the grades would take care of themselves if the teaching was good. Finally, I had to face the fact that the teaching could only be as good as the grading system, which made it impossible for me to continue the practice of averaged grades. I *had* to find an alternative. There had to be a better system—one that actually helps students. As my doubts about averaging grades grew, I hoped the faculty as a whole would move toward a better system. In *Fair Isn't Always Equal*, experienced former educator and author Rick Wormeli (2006) clearly calls for teachers to engage in candid discussions about grading:

> There are some aspects of teaching that we keep in cages in hopes they will never escape. . . . We don't share our concerns with our own grading approach or that of a colleague's often, and we don't spend time with each other determining the meaning of a C, an A, or discussing what constitutes a 3.5 on a rubric. . . . The day is upon us, however. It's time to talk about grades, grading, and report cards openly, if we haven't before, questioning assumptions, embracing alternatives, and focusing on the promise of what teaching and learning can be. (p. 89)

One of the most difficult challenges professionals in any field face is overwhelming evidence that a common, long-standing practice is actually harmful to those it is intended to serve. It took me years to get to a point when I confronted the problem of averaged grades. It would be unreasonable to expect all my colleagues to arrive at this point simultaneously. So for a while, I accepted the fact that I was on my own. Ironically, I owed my freedom to try something new to the very autonomy that made changing the school policy and culture on grades so difficult.

The Promise of the Student-Centered Approach

Moffett and Wagner (1992) believe teachers can trust students to want to learn when students are sure *learning* (rather than compliance) is the teachers' first concern. They urge teachers to be partners with students in learning and to "concentrate on keeping the ownership of the work and the goal-setting with the student" (Moffett & Wagner, 1992, p. 251). Students don't need endless essays and tests to know when they are making progress. "If the teacher is freed from emceeing to circulate and observe, then good evaluation becomes possible without resorting to special activities that detract from learning" (Moffett & Wagner, 1992, pp. 243–244).

I have seen this to be true in my own experience. While I was English department chair at Newtown High School (2001 to 2011), I remember Abi Marks, a teacher in the department, asking to observe one of my classes. The gist of her comment afterward was that the class just seemed to run itself. There came a time when I visited Abi's classroom and made essentially the same comment about her students. It takes a considerable amount of planning and preparation for a class to run itself, but when it does, the experience is immensely satisfying for both students and teacher.

This sounds wonderful, but how do we know how students are actually doing? Christi Alper (2018), an experienced high school science teacher, grapples with this issue in her own teaching. She wanted to use a student-centered approach called inquiry-based learning because the research convinced her of the benefits for students, but she had a hard time letting go of direct instruction and sharing control of their learning with her students. Alper (2018) is candid about her struggle to let go of traditional teaching methods as well as her determination to do so:

> As an educator, I felt that I needed to be in control of student behavior. . . . I worried about whether they would arrive at the right answer, but with most inquiry-based learning the questions can have many solutions. So I needed to let go of some rigidity and embrace the freedom of students taking ownership of their knowledge formation. . . . My students were still held accountable for their education because they were required to produce evidence for the completion of the case study regardless of their chosen solution. This shift offered me the time to differentiate and support their individual needs. I could check in with students who were struggling to progress through the inquiry and ask thought-provoking questions to challenge more advanced students' understanding. . . . Wrestling with messy, open-ended questions allowed students to understand the content more deeply.

It's a natural part of the learning process for us as human beings to toggle back and forth between what we want to achieve, what we have achieved, and where we started. This healthy process allows us to know there is more to learn and the satisfaction of making progress. Students should be active participants in this natural process in school just as much as in other parts of their lives, including sports, music, being a friend and family member, and so on. In a teacher-directed setting, students figure out how to get good grades from the teacher rather than working in partnership with the teacher to figure out who they are, what they're good at, and what they need to work on. Students are wizards of efficiency at getting through assignments when there is no personal investment. I have heard a student lament that the last time he read a book he liked was in fifth grade, and I have heard a student brag that she did none of the reading and still earned an A in the class. The uncomfortable truth is that traditional practices produce unintended consequences.

A student-centered approach recognizes that teachers can count on students to know a lot about how they're doing. Moffett and Wagner (1992) are clear that a partnership approach to assessment is not "anything goes," writing, "Let all parties know that all activities are assessed all the time, but don't ever give the impression that the assessment is intended for anything but help and encouragement" (p. 246).

Moffett has long been a highly influential figure in the world of education, and he was far from the only one to advocate for this approach. In an article for the National

Staff Development Council, Rick Stiggins and Jan Chappuis (2006) call for changes in assessment practices that would include students in the decision-making loop about what they should know and how they should demonstrate that knowledge: "Students must be taught the skills they need to be in control of their own ultimate academic success: self-assessment and goal setting, reflection, keeping track of and sharing their learning" (p. 13). Through years of service as a teacher of teachers and as director of the Centers for Classroom Assessment and Performance Assessment at the Northwest Regional Educational Laboratory, and through publication of articles and books, such as *The Perfect Assessment System*, Stiggins (2017) has steadfastly argued for an overhaul of assessment in the United States and asked the hard questions. These are the same questions that inspired me to make the changes in my teaching practice that have resulted in this book: What if we were able as educators to let go of what we've done in the past and try something that is better for students? What if we could integrate learning and assessment so naturally and thoroughly that the latter never interferes with the former? What if we ask students to engage in reflection and self-assessment and treat their findings with respect? What if the observations a teacher makes while students are working in collaborative groups were given serious consideration as a source of information for education policy?

So many researchers, theorists, and consultants have done the hard work and shared what they learned in articles, books, videos, podcasts, and presentations. The research is abundant and clear: students benefit from a student-centered approach. Yet policymakers remain fainthearted about tackling traditional practices. Christi Alper (2018) speaks for all of us when she admits that it can feel uncomfortable to share control of learning with students. But the reward for enduring the discomfort of change is the great satisfaction of seeing renewed joy in students as they learn and develop as individuals. We can get there, one teacher and one classroom at a time. When teacher and student work together to assess progress, it's what Moffett and Wagner (1992) call the *totality of a student's work* that matters, not one assignment or another.

With all this in mind, I have identified three components of a student-centered approach to evaluation that can mitigate the consequences of traditional grading and make your classroom a safe haven of true learning. Instead of grading assignments and reporting the average, you can:

1. Use formative assessment to provide timely, specific feedback on student work

2. Differentiate the learning process and product through approaches such as inquiry and performance-based learning to meet individual student needs with flexible adaptation of task and sequence (the student-centered teacher recognizes that each student arrives in the classroom with a unique combination of prior knowledge and experience)

3. Integrate reflection and self-assessment into the evaluation process, working with your students as a partner to evaluate progress toward achievement of learning goals

Next, we'll discuss those three important components of a student-centered approach to evaluation, each of which contributes to a climate of mutual respect and trust in the classroom and to positive connections with each student's home.

Timely, Specific Feedback

Robert J. Marzano (2000, 2013, 2017) is an education researcher who tends to work in the realm of meta-analysis. Marzano (2000, 2013, 2017) is careful to present objectively only what substantial research supports. I was initially struck by two concise, clear assertions he makes a point of including in *Transforming Classroom Grading*:

1. The most important purpose for grades is to provide information or feedback to students and parents.

2. The best referencing system for grades is content-specific learning goals: a criterion-referenced approach. (Marzano, 2000, p. 23)

Implicit in Marzano's (2000, 2013, 2017) findings is a truly transformative idea: feedback and grades are not necessarily the same thing. You can consider a grade a form of feedback, but it's a very limited form. Most of the time, feedback that helps students make progress toward achievement of learning goals needs to take a more substantial form, including comments on what students have accomplished and advice about how to proceed. In an article called "Do You Have a 'Stop Doing' List?" Chris Jakicic (2019) couldn't make this concept plainer: "We need to stop grading formative and common formative assessments. If the purpose of these assessments is to know what students still need to learn, grading them signals that the opportunity for learning has closed." Instead, Jakicic (2019) urges teachers to provide feedback to students that helps them see what their work reveals about what they have learned; then students should receive opportunities to be part of figuring out their next steps. Only at the end of the marking period would students need to show progress in the form of a grade. And this grade should report where students are rather than where they have been. As Marzano (2000) notes:

> It would make little sense to combine all the test scores for a given student (by computing an average score for example) during a unit, because this might penalize the student for his lack of knowledge at the beginning of the unit. (p. 22)

Marzano (2017, 2018) pursues this line of thinking in books such as *The New Art and Science of Teaching* and *Making Classroom Assessments Reliable and Valid*. While frequent, specific feedback is essential to the student's progress all the time, the only point at which it makes sense to express the student's achievement as a grade is at the end of a marking period. Grades on individual assignments not only are a waste of time but also could be misleading.

What might have seemed like a radical idea when Marzano first articulated it in 2000 has gained support. For example, in an article called "Standards-Based Grading Will Improve Education," Marco A. Muñoz and Thomas R. Guskey (2015) concur with Marzano's beliefs about grading:

> It is time to change our traditional approaches for grading and reporting in our nation's schools. The scaling-up process of the suggested approach for grading and reporting will enhance student learning. Reporting must be valid, reliable, fair, and useful; nothing less should be expected if we want to link grading and reporting with students' mastery of content and practice standards. Standards-based grading and reporting has much more to offer over the traditional scattershot approach. (p. 68)

In *Grading From the Inside Out*, Tom Schimmer (2016) makes the point that grades neutralize feedback. Marzano's findings are underscored by Schimmer's (2016) work to help educators understand how failure of grading practices to keep up with the movement toward standards-based teaching has produced dissonance between what students do and what teachers report about their progress. Schimmer is interested in the mindsets that have to change in order for teaching and reporting to be in alignment. In an interview with Justin Baeder (2016) on Principal Center Radio, Schimmer points out that students and parents need and want accurate information about student proficiency. It's important to note that, according to Muñoz and Guskey (2015), "Early results from pilot implementation indicate that teachers and parents favor this standards-based reporting over the traditional approach" (p. 68). Teachers might persist in traditional grading practices in the belief that this is what parents expect, but recent research suggests this is not the case (Muñoz & Guskey, 2015).

The important thing is to enable students to toggle between learning goals, which remain constant throughout the year for all students, and individual assignments that could change to meet each student's individual needs. Traditional grading asks students, parents, counselors, and college admission offices to infer progress toward achievement of learning goals from grades on assignments. Grades on assignments are an intermediate step in the process of reporting student progress. Teachers can express progress toward achievement of learning goals as a number on a scale of 1–10 or 1–100. Let's say you want to report how a student is doing with applying the scientific method to experiments and writing up the results. You could grade a bunch of practice sheets, data-collection forms, quizzes, and, ultimately, an independent experiment and report that demonstrates the student's use of the scientific method. Or, you could observe the student during the learning process, make suggestions while an experiment is actually in progress, listen in while the student plans the independent experiment with feedback from a collaborative group, give feedback on a draft of the big lab report, and finally, sit down with the student, look at all the work, decide the student has demonstrated substantial progress, and enter a 9 out of 10 for that learning goal.

The learning goals you select should already be familiar to students and parents. Any well-written set of goals that are both challenging and accessible will work. According to Robert J. Marzano (2013):

> Any system that organizes statements of what students are expected to know and be able to do enhances student learning because it provides clarity to students and teachers alike. Educators should feel free to create their own systems or adapt those that others have proposed.

I worked primarily with sophomores and juniors. The sophomores take a state-mandated test, and the juniors take standardized tests from the College Board, so for both groups, I selected test-related learning goals. I also included some items from the Partnership for 21st Century Learning (2019) framework definitions for "Communication and Collaboration" (p. 5). And, finally, I added standards for spoken language an interdisciplinary group of teachers within my school district developed. Taken together, there were two dozen learning goals for each course, which proved to be a reasonable number. Selecting learning goals in this way firmly connects your classroom and the work you ask students to do with what the school community already values. If there are any concerns about your departure from traditional teacher-centered instructional methods, you can allay them more easily when it's clear that everyone shares the same familiar goals.

Flexible Sequencing of Tasks, Projects, and Performances

Each task, project, and performance you design for and with students should pass two tests. First, it should provide a rich opportunity for students to make progress toward achievement of learning goals. Second, it should be flexible enough to fit the interests and needs of individual students and groups of students. Chapters 3 (page 39) and 4 (page 61) provide detailed discussion of enduring tasks, projects, and performances that I came back to again and again, both to teach skills and to give students a way to demonstrate what they had learned. Gathering information about students' interests, needs, and progress begins early, continues all year, and is an integral part of the flexible teaching and learning sequence. The initial sequence might look something like this.

- Students complete a self-assessment chart, indicating their current level of progress toward achieving their learning goals, as well as a written survey of their history with the grade-level or course material.

- Students complete an initial formative assessment on a topic of interest that indicates their current capacity to apply knowledge and skills central to the grade level or course.

- The teacher provides detailed feedback on the formative assessment, including suggestions about ways to pursue additional information or insight into the student-selected topic of interest. The teacher also sets up an anecdotal record for each student and begins making notes on interests and needs.

- The teacher introduces the first unit of study, topic, readings, and skills the grade-level or course curriculum requires, using awareness of student interests to create multiple access points.

- The teacher launches a task with the whole class, using collaborative reading strategies to work through course material, including key concepts and skills.

- Students participate in the task, responding to prompts in a course notebook, sharing passages from this provisional writing, and reflecting on the process. The teacher listens to what students share and uses this material to identify individual needs as well as the disposition of the whole class.

- The teacher launches a project that will help students develop the knowledge and skills they need to achieve learning goals.

- Students engage in the first round of planning with collaborative group members, focusing on how to integrate their own interests and needs into their approach to the project. The teacher circulates to listen, answer questions, and make suggestions.

- Students work on the project at home, share their progress with group members in class, and give and get feedback. The teacher once again circulates to listen, answer questions, and make suggestions.

- The teacher calls for a complete draft of the project, giving students a range of several days to email or hand in the draft.

- The teacher logs the drafts as they come in, provides detailed feedback, makes notes in the anecdotal records, and meets with students who are having problems. Students use the feedback to make modifications.

- The teacher launches the performance phase of the sequence, providing students with a self-assessment instrument to guide their planning and progress.
- Students plan their performances with collaborative group members while the teacher circulates to listen, answer questions, and make suggestions.
- Students present their performances while giving and getting feedback from class members.
- The teacher completes an assessment of each performance, which he or she then shares with students, and adds notes to the anecdotal record.

The trick is to find a balance between launching a task, project, or performance with the entire class and then modifying to meet individual and group needs. Taking a flexible, student-centered approach doesn't mean the curriculum goes out the window; it just means you keep individual students in mind when designing the opportunities they need to develop knowledge and skills and make progress toward achievement of learning goals. Each task, project, or performance should generate work students care about and are willing to revise, perhaps multiple times, to get it just right. And students need to be active partners with the teacher in figuring out how to tailor each task, project, or performance so it will fit their specific interests, strengths, and needs.

Flexible sequencing moves back and forth between teacher and students as the teacher launches a task, project, or performance with the class as a whole, keeping individual interests in mind, and then students work as individuals or in collaborative groups to plan how to tackle the task, project, or performance. This approach to lesson design owes much to the practice of differentiation. Education author and presenter Laurie Robinson Sammons (2017) clearly and concisely summarizes the differences in thinking between traditional and differentiated lesson design (see figure 5.1, page 102). The rigidity of a traditional approach stands in stark contrast to the flexibility that differentiation offers.

The goal is always the highest levels of learning possible, but the route to get there may differ for each student. Allowing them some say in this route is key. John McCarthy (2015) is an education consultant whose mission in life is to appreciate and support students' voices in their learning. McCarthy's work is based on what he learned from the work of Carol Ann Tomlinson and from his collaboration with Susan Allan, who, like Tomlinson, is a veteran advocate of differentiation. The updated edition of Tomlinson's (2017) *How to Differentiate Instruction in Academically Diverse Classrooms* is essential reading on this topic. When McCarthy (2015) writes, "The core of differentiation is a relationship between teachers and students," he sums up the fundamental connection between differentiation and the student-centered approach advocated in this book.

Traditional	Differentiated
"Teaching and covering content are my first priorities."	"Since student learning is my focus, the way I teach is contingent upon student needs and fidelity to a guaranteed and viable curriculum."
"Learning goals are the same for all students."	"Learning targets are adjusted by student needs, but the goal is grade-level proficiency and beyond."
"The textbook is the foundation for information."	"The world is our classroom, and we use multiple resources for learning."
"Whole-classroom instruction is most beneficial and manageable for me."	"Students learn through whole-group, small-group, individual, and flexible-learning groups on a consistent basis."
"All students are expected to complete the same learning tasks."	"I intentionally design a variety of tasks so students do, show, and tell their understanding in different ways."

Source: Sammons, 2017.

Figure 5.1: Different philosophies of instruction.

If a student or a group of students needs to let go of a project that just isn't working and try something new, flexible sequencing of tasks and projects makes this simple. For example, if a student comes in from another school district and has already studied whatever is going on in the class, no problem. Students might be working on somewhat different tasks at times, and, depending on their needs, some students may do more than others. Once you make the shift from averaging grades to reporting progress toward achievement of learning goals, it doesn't matter that students might not complete exactly the same assignments or exactly the same number of assignments. That's because the focus is on what the student is learning rather than how many assignments the student turns in. With *flexible sequencing*, the teacher assigns work, and the students turn it in much as usual, the big difference being that the system is set up to help students when they have a problem instead of punishing them for not adhering to due dates that are, essentially, arbitrary.

For many of my twenty-five years of teaching, my gradebook adhered to the traditional grading system, and looked something like figure 5.2. I used a point system that emphasized major projects more than provisional work, but I did not distinguish between work done early in the marking period and work done later. At the end of the marking period, I added up the points each student earned and divided that number by the total points possible. I liked this system better than weighted test, project, and homework grades because it was easier for students to figure out where they stood. The total points system may have been more user-friendly, but it was still

	Summer reading 20 points	Journal entries 50 points	Personal essay 100 points	Argument essay 100 points	Literary analysis 100 points	Narrative or poem 50 points	Reading exam 100 points
Student A	20	50	95	90	90	50	100
Student B	20	45	85	85	80	45	90
Student C	15	35	80	75	75	40	70
Student D	10	30	70	70	65	25	65
Student F	0	0	50	0	0	50	100

Figure 5.2: Example of a traditional gradebook.

fraught with all the problems of grading each assignment and deriving final grades from averaged grades.

Once I stopped grading individual assignments and focused instead on students' progress toward achieving learning goals, they needed to know that I would still keep track of what they planned and completed. They needed to know that they would be hearing from me if I didn't hear from them. Instead of a gradebook, I maintained a log of student work, like the example in figure 5.3 (page 104).

Anna's row in the log represents the type of student who turned everything in—often early—and would write some innocuous personal essay to get the grade. But too often the Annas of the world have a difficult situation at home they are not ready to write about. A motivated student could get started on the literary analysis with the expectation that it would reflect some independent research, and save the personal essay for later, when there might be some benefit from writing about the difficult situation. All I had to do was make a quick note about the personal essay and enter the actual date when I received a complete draft of the literary analysis.

As for Brett, Colleen, and Don, they represent the many students who were used to doing what the teacher asked and turning work in on time. In fact, this type of student is okay with being told what to do because they have figured out it is much easier to do what you're told than to figure out what to do on your own. They would be so concerned about not getting a grade on every assignment that they would work up the courage to meet with me to discuss this. This meeting would give me a chance to go into more detail and to be more personally reassuring about the benefits to them of student-centered evaluation. These students would initially have some

	Summer reading	Journal entries	Personal essay	Argument essay
Anna	September 7	September 20	Start literary analysis	September 22
Brett	September 7	September 20	September 16	September 24
Colleen	September 7	September 20	September 20	September 27
Don	September 7	September 20	September 20	October 4
Phil		September 20	Done (private)	Op-ed for school newspaper

	Literary analysis	Narrative or poem	Reading exam
Anna	September 14	October 25	100
Brett	October 16	October 27	95
Colleen	October 16	October 28	90
Don	October 18	October 29	90
Phil	October 16	September 20	100

Figure 5.3: Example of using a gradebook as a student work log.

trouble coming up with topics for research and writing, again providing me with opportunities to listen and learn and help them figure out what they wanted to know more about. As students worked in their collaborative groups, I had time to circulate, listen, answer questions, and offer suggestions.

Phil's row in the chart represents the students who resist the pressures of teachers and administrators to comply and conform. Phil would find a way to test me, such as not turning in the evidence of summer reading the English department required of all students. I would have given students time in class to write journal entries about their summer reading and share them by reading passages aloud. Phil's participation in the class activity would have given me the first inkling that he was in fact an avid reader. That left me with a choice: I could enter "Not done" in the log for the formal evidence of summer reading or I could accept the in-class evidence and enter the date. A moment like this is critical for the partnership between student and teacher. Even after I indicated my trust, the Phils of the world might continue to test, perhaps by saying he had written the personal essay but could not turn it in because the topic was too personal. Such a student might be abusing my trust or might be too used to resisting pressure to follow rules and directions to behave; otherwise, I would take

Phil at his word and simply enter "Done" in the log, hoping that the testing would stop and our student-teacher partnership would begin to thrive.

The flexibility inherent in student-centered evaluation makes it possible to offer trust instead of deducting points for the missing essay. It's satisfying to see any student succeed and especially so when the student is not used to success. Over twenty-five years of teaching, I have found that things turn out better if my initial response to a student who seems out of line is to offer trust. On the very few occasions when students have taken advantage of that initial offer of trust, it doesn't take long to figure out what's going on and respond accordingly.

Shared Evaluation of Student Progress

When we think of evaluation, the image that comes automatically to mind is a teacher sitting alone at the kitchen table, dutifully grading a pile of papers late into the night. The hours are long, the sacrifice is great, the intentions are good. But a dedicated teacher can put his or her time and energy to better use by sitting down with a student and having a conversation about how it's going. Students don't need grades on their papers. What they need is feedback on how they're doing while they're doing it and opportunities to discuss their progress. And these discussions should not be a one-way street; the student shouldn't simply be listening while the teacher talks about progress and grades. There needs to be an active back-and-forth discussion of teacher and student listening to each other and speaking honestly about the student's needs while sharing pride and excitement about the student's strengths.

Scott Marion (n.d.), executive director of the National Center for the Improvement of Educational Assessment, reminds us that what he refers to as "student-led" assessment is nothing new, pointing back in time to John Dewey and, more recently, the work of Theodore Sizer and the Coalition of Essential Schools. Marion (n.d.) writes:

> We should actively engage students in their own learning and assessment as early as possible because of the considerable benefits in learning academic content and skills and especially for building the kinds of dispositions (e.g., 21st Century Skills) we hope to see in all students.

Marion (n.d.) further emphasizes how important it is for students "to develop the self-regulatory and metacognitive skills that they will need to monitor their own learning." Imagine teacher and student sitting together, heads bent over the student's notebook, the most recent project up on the laptop screen, making entries on the student's chart of learning goals, the pencil in the student's hand as often as in the teacher's. This image is the reality of shared evaluation of student progress. Meeting with students takes time, but that time becomes available when teachers let go of the unnecessary work of grading everything and use the time instead to talk with students.

I devoted extra time and thought to the first handouts I distributed to students and parents that departed from averaged grades. I wanted it to be clear: I was trying something new. But I also wanted to allay concerns without too much second-guessing. After much revision, my explanation (see figure 5.4) amounted to less than half a page in the handouts.

Students earn points for engaging in the process of learning and for making progress toward achieving learning goals. Students can demonstrate progress with written and spoken performance as well as with their logs and portfolio documents. In addition, during each marking period, there will be one or two reading exams that combine an essay prompt with objective questions about texts, literary terms, and conventions of print. Each marking period will conclude with a student-teacher conference based on log, portfolio, exam, and a reflective essay called "State of the Student." I expect students to be active participants in the evaluation process. Students earn points for progress toward achievement of each learning goal:

10 points = Documented mastery
9 points = Major documented progress
8 points = Documented progress
7 points = Documented attempt

I then convert each student's progress toward achievement of learning goals into a conventional grade percentage derived from the number of points the student earns of the total possible:

Performance Learning Goals: 150 possible points
(10 points each for fifteen standards)

Collaboration Learning Goals: 80 possible points
(10 points each for eight standards)

Reading Exams: 50–100 possible points

State of the Student: 50 possible points

Total: 330–380 possible points

Figure 5.4: Teacher's evaluation process explanation.

One of the most important components of a student-centered approach to evaluation is the student's active participation. Early in the first marking period, before the unit actually begins, ask students to evaluate their current level of progress toward achievement of learning goals. I have found that these self-evaluations were, on the whole, honest and accurate. For example, early in the year, a fifth grader's self-evaluation of mathematics goals might have entries such as those in figure 5.5.

Check the box that most accurately represents your current level of achievement:

10 = I have mastered this goal
9 = I still need a little help from the teacher, but I can do this mostly on my own
8 = I made good progress toward this goal last year
7 = I can do this with teacher feedback and support
? = I have not been introduced to this goal

Mathematics goal	10	9	8	7	?
Use mathematics to solve real-world problems.		✓			
Work in a group to solve challenging problems.	✓				
Use a variety of estimation strategies.			✓		
Round whole numbers and decimals.		✓			
Add, subtract, multiply, and divide with decimals and whole numbers.			✓		
Add, subtract, multiply, and divide with fractions.				✓	
Solve an equation with one variable.					✓
Collect information from graphs and tables.		✓			
Measure angles with a protractor.			✓		
Make accurate measurements using a ruler, scale, and thermometer.		✓			
Use data to predict outcomes.					✓

Figure 5.5: Sample fifth-grade self-evaluation chart for mathematics learning goals.

Visit **go.SolutionTree.com/instruction** *for a free reproducible version of this figure.*

Of course, in the initial self-evaluation, a few students may exaggerate their level of achievement; you might see a long row of checks under 10, but this can be cleared up with a little good-natured feedback. A companion problem might be a long row of checks under ?, which would also signal a need for some conversation about the student's mathematics experience. I've found most students are realistic about where they stand. Asking students to provide detailed information about their progress toward achievement of learning goals sends a clear message: evaluation will be a partnership between students and the teacher. Students need to know the teacher will acknowledge and respect what they have already accomplished. The baseline self-evaluation makes it plain that no one is starting from scratch.

In a fifth-grade classroom, self-evaluation charts will be necessary for English language arts as well as mathematics. Depending on the grade-level expectations, students may also need charts for science and social studies. Learning goals related to group work are essential in any student-centered setting. As you set up the charts, just make sure you have a doable number of learning goals and that the wording of each goal is clear to students. Try to focus on large goals rather than isolating individual skills. The learning goals should remain the same for each student all year, so the initial self-evaluation should indicate that there's work to be done as well as much that has already been achieved.

There may be some situations that call for an update in students' baseline scores. I had to deal with some procrastinators and one student who did not turn in any written work. After consultations with the student, parents, and the guidance counselor, I decided it would send the clearest message if I entered a zero for learning goals for the lack of written work (meaning that the student did fail), but this was the only instance I used the zero. The procrastinators got the message when they saw their scores related to group work fall to 6 or 7 on a ten-point scale.

Toward the end of the first marking period, you will need to set aside time to meet with each student to review feedback the student has already received, discuss any issues, note progress toward achievement of learning goals, and decide what score best represents that progress. Because you've been sharing feedback throughout, there shouldn't be any surprises during this meeting. Use figure 5.6 to record such scores each marking period. The *Student Evaluation* column is for the student's initial self-evaluation. The scores for the first marking period will likely be similar to the student's self-evaluation. The reason for this is that it's natural for students to encounter new material and increased expectations as they move from one grade level to another. When grades are averaged across an entire marking period, this natural dip related to the learning curve can have a detrimental impact on the student's overall scores, which is yet another reason not to average grades. The final marking period scores should reflect the student's current level of achievement, nothing more and nothing less. If the student has not yet had an opportunity to work on a particular skill, the box can simply be left blank, which is the case in the example in figure 5.6 with the goals related to equations and predicting outcomes.

Some learning goals may be specific to a particular grade level or subject area. Others might apply more broadly. For example, teachers might introduce the spoken communication learning goals in figure 5.7 (page 110) in fifth grade, with the students developing them in middle school and fine-tuning them in high school.

As you review each student's work, you'll want to see evidence in the course notebook that the student has participated actively in tasks, but the main focus will be on what projects and performances show about his or her progress toward achieving learning goals. The projects provide formative opportunities for students to engage with new knowledge and skills, and the performances provide summative

Mathematics goal	Student evaluation	Marking period 1	Marking period 2	Marking period 3	Marking period 4
Use mathematics to solve real-world problems.	9	9			
Work in a group to solve challenging problems.	10	10			
Use a variety of estimation strategies.	8	9			
Round whole numbers and decimals.	9	10			
Add, subtract, multiply, and divide with decimals and whole numbers.	8	9			
Add, subtract, multiply, and divide with fractions.	7	7			
Solve an equation with one variable.	?				
Collect information from graphs and tables.	9	8			
Measure angles with a protractor.	8	8			
Make accurate measurements using a ruler, scale, and thermometer.	9	9			
Use data to predict outcomes.	?				

Figure 5.6: Sample fifth-grade student progress log for mathematics learning goals.

Visit **go.SolutionTree.com/instruction** *for a free reproducible version of this figure.*

opportunities for students to demonstrate their progress toward achieving multiple learning goals. Teachers should review both projects and performances, along with the feedback students received on them, during the student-teacher evaluation conference. If there is an area where the student is having difficulty, you'll be able to say,

Spoken communication goal	Student evaluation	Marking period 1	Marking period 2	Marking period 3	Marking period 4
Make word choices to engage the audience, and use terminology specific to the topic.					
Adjust pace and volume to enhance communication (controlled, energetic, purposeful).					
Convey information and ideas with authority and originality.					
Make purposeful use of eye contact, stance, and demeanor to engage the audience.					
Organize spoken and visual components in an engaging sequence with smooth transitions.					

Figure 5.7: Sample student progress log for spoken communication learning goals.

Visit **go.SolutionTree.com/instruction** *for a free reproducible version of this figure.*

"Don't be afraid of a low score now. Your scores will build throughout the year, so a low score just lets us know what you need to work on." Students are accountable for the work they need to do to make and demonstrate progress. But they are also free to enjoy learning for its own intrinsic rewards. And you are free to take a teaching approach that makes more of your time and energy directly available to students.

Because evaluation is based on evidence of progress in the work each student does over a period of time (rather than averaged grades on assignments), it's important to save their work in some form of folder. For elementary students who might need help with organization, collect work in folders kept in the classroom, where both student and teacher have easy access. As students move on to secondary school, shift more responsibility to them to manage a collection that will likely combine a folder of handwritten work and digital storage. You can save projects students send to you electronically on a flash drive or on Google Drive (https://google.com/drive). This transfer will make it easy for you to access a student's work at home as well as in the classroom. In addition to projects, the digital folder you maintain for each student should include an *anecdotal record*. This is where you make notes as you get to know the student; these notes will help you tailor tasks and projects to meet his or her individual needs. As the example in figure 5.8 shows, you can select several learning goals to track in detail. The goals might be the same for the whole class, or they might differ from one student to another. The anecdotal record also gives you a place to store comments on student work you may want to return to as well as suggestions from student-teacher conferences.

Goal	September	October	November	December	January
Collaboration mathematics: Work in a group to solve challenging mathematics problems.					
English language arts: Use quotation marks around quoted material, and include author, title, and date of source.					
Spoken communication: Organize spoken and visual components in an engaging sequence with smooth transitions.					
Comments and suggestions:					

Figure 5.8: Example of an anecdotal record.

I invested a lot of time in this record the first semester but less in the second semester after I knew my students better. These anecdotal records were a great help in preparing for parent conferences and making placement recommendations.

When it's time to report progress for the first marking period, email the anecdotal record to each student, along with the guidelines for writing the first State of the Student report. For this initial report, ask students to focus on their progress toward achievement of learning goals for collaboration and to write detailed responses to two questions: (1) What concerns or questions do you have about your work for this course? and (2) What can the teacher do to make the course more useful, meaningful, and enjoyable? Then it is simply a matter of student and teacher putting their heads together to go over the documents and decide what to enter in the student's evaluation chart toward achievement of learning goals (see figure 5.6, page 109, for an example). The student will complete the first column with his or her baseline self-assessment from the beginning of the year. During your conference, you and the student can agree not to evaluate learning goals for which the student had limited opportunity to demonstrate progress. Because scores will build over the year (rather than being averaged), there is no need for a student to feel anxious about a low score at the beginning of the year. The evaluation conference provides an opportunity to share understanding of the student's strengths and areas for growth and to celebrate what the student has already accomplished. As you talk with each student, you can add two or three specific suggestions to the anecdotal record, which you can email again after the conference, so you and students stay on the same page about next steps.

As students become comfortable with the process of evaluating their progress toward achievement of course learning goals, the time for conferences will lessen. With secondary students, the last round of conferences could even take place via email. As one student wrote, "The most rewarding aspect of this course is the opportunity to grade ourselves so that we aren't always stressed out with our grades. The grading system makes our class branch out and really explore our minds for interesting new ways to write essays and work collaboratively" (R. Schmidt, personal communication, June 2010).

In my school's electronic gradebook, I would enter a full description of each learning goal (see figure 5.9) and a shortened version that was compatible with the printed grade report format (see figure 5.10, page 114). The electronic grade program calculates marking-period grades in exactly the same way, whether what the teacher enters in those long horizontal rows is a marking period's worth of grades on teacher-directed assignments or a record of the student's progress toward achievement of course learning goals. The difference is not in how the teacher handles the numbers but in what the numbers represent. Instead of an average of all the student work attempted over the course of a marking period, the student-centered approach shows where the student stands at the end of the marking period. The focus is not on compliance, but on individual growth over time.

Analysis: Analyze and interpret samples of good writing, identifying and explaining an author's use of rhetorical strategies and techniques.

Application: Apply effective strategies and techniques in students' own writing.

Argument: Create and sustain arguments based on readings, research, and personal experience.

Audience: Revise a work to make it suitable for a different audience.

Central idea: Produce expository, analytical, and argumentative compositions that introduce a complex central idea, and develop it with appropriate evidence drawn from primary and secondary source material, cogent explanations, and clear transitions.

Citation: Demonstrate understanding of the conventions of citing primary and secondary source material.

Image: Analyze image as text.

Process: Move effectively through the stages of the writing process with careful attention to inquiry and research, drafting, revising, editing, and review.

Purpose: Write for a variety of purposes.

References: Evaluate and incorporate reference documents into researched papers.

Reflection: Write thoughtfully about their own process of composition.

Style: Demonstrate understanding and mastery of standard written English as well as stylistic maturity in students' own writing.

Community: Act responsibly with the interests of the larger community in mind.

Criticism: Deal positively with praise, setbacks, and criticism.

Diversity: Demonstrate the ability to work effectively with diverse teams.

Feedback: Be open and responsive to new and diverse perspectives; incorporate group input and feedback into the work.

Flexibility: Exercise flexibility and willingness to be helpful in making necessary compromises to accomplish a common goal.

Goals: Set and meet high standards and goals for delivering quality work on time.

Responsibility: Assume shared responsibility for collaborative work.

Roles: Adapt to varied roles and responsibilities.

Diction: Make word choices to engage the audience, and make fluent use of terminology specific to the topic.

Dynamics: Modulate pace and volume to enhance communication (controlled, energetic, purposeful).

Information: Convey information and ideas with authority and originality.

Nonverbal: Make purposeful use of eye contact, stance, and demeanor to engage audience.

Sequence: Organize spoken and visual components in an engaging sequence with skillful transitions.

Figure 5.9: Full description of each learning goal.

Analysis	Application	Argument	Audience	Central idea	Citation	Image	Process	Purpose	References	Reflection	Style	Community
9	10	10	9	10	9		9	10	10	9	10	
7	8	9	9	9	5		7	8	9	8	9	
8	8	10	9	9	8		6	9	10	10	8	

Criticism	Diversity	Feedback	Flexibility	Goals	Responsibility	Roles	Diction	Dynamics	Information	Nonverbal	Sequence
8	9	9	8	10	10	9	8	8	10	8	9
8	9	9	9	5	8	8	10	10	8	10	9
9	8	9	8	9	9	7	8	6	9	7	9

Figure 5.10: Shortened version of a school's electronic gradebook.

Each row of numbers tells a story—from the outstanding student who recognized she had a hard time accepting criticism and whose anxiety about public speaking initially prevented her from giving her good ideas the rousing delivery they deserved, to the student whose weakness was analytical writing but whose engaging speaking skills served as a role model for his peers, to the student who faced the fact that his habit of procrastinating was preventing him from making the progress he was capable of. I confess, the first time I reported students' progress toward learning goals instead of averaging assignment grades, I was anxious when grades went out. Even though I was pleased with the quality of the information I included in the online gradebook, I couldn't help thinking there would be some parental concerns. However, the parents as well as students continued to accept the student-centered approach. It was also at this point the principal asked me to stop by his office. My heart sank, thinking a parent might have gone straight to him. "Everything's fine," he said. "I'm just interested in what you're doing."

Even when student-centered evaluation is going well, you'll want confirmation that students' progress toward achievement of learning goals is consistent with their performance on a traditional assessment. For elementary students, make this an opportunity to practice with released items from grade-appropriate standardized tests.

Just make sure students understand that you're asking them to work on traditional test materials to show how they're doing from a different perspective and to practice traditional test-taking skills.

For secondary students, make up a traditional subject-area exam specific to material you've been working on in class. For my students, I was careful to generate exams that required some review but mostly rewarded students for what they had learned about key concepts and important skills. I constructed the exams so students only needed to recognize key terms rather than having to recall them. This required providing a word bank for questions about terms and including passages from the course readings for analysis, rather than expecting students to recall specific details. When I asked students for comments about the exam, the majority said they liked it because the questions were fair, and the formal exam gave them a chance to see how much they'd learned from another perspective.

When you look at the scores, you want to see most students within a few points of the average of their scores on learning goals. I noticed a disparity between the two for a few students. Their exam scores were quite a bit lower than the averages of their scores on learning goals. I hoped it was because they didn't bother to review key terms or because they were anxious about taking an exam. In these few cases, I offered a *form B* of the exam, giving those who didn't study a second chance to do so and using familiarity with the exam format to lower anxiety. Invariably, the results dispelled my concerns. If there had been more than a few instances of disparity between the exam score and the average of scores on learning goals, the problem would have been mine. I would ask myself, "Did the exam accurately represent what students worked on in class? Was the exam written well enough so students were not lured into incorrect or incomplete responses by ambiguously worded questions and prompts? Did too much emphasis on affective skills and not enough on academic performance (or vice versa) skew students' learning goal scores?"

I asked students to self-assess their exam essays and usually agreed with their assessment. Teachers can use the same simple rubric in figure 5.11 for a wide variety of essay questions.

Demonstrated attempt	**Demonstrated progress**	**Demonstrated mastery**
Discussion is general, and support is absent or vague. Errors are frequent and interfere with meaning.	Discussion is thoughtful, and support is relevant. Errors are few and do not interfere with meaning.	Discussion is insightful and original, and support is both relevant and varied. Errors are rare.

Figure 5.11: Sample rubric for essay questions.

I worked with a comprehensive online grading system that included grades on assignments as well as grades for each marking period, each semester, and the course as a whole. Typically, assignment grades accumulate until the marking period ends, and the teacher averages all grades to produce the grade for the marking period. The student-centered evaluation system produces scores for progress toward achievement of learning goals rather than grades on individual assignments, but you don't want the pages in the online grading system empty all marking period. To prevent this, roll the final scores for one marking period into the next, sending the message that students don't start over with each new marking period. Instead of starting over, students begin each marking period with what they have already achieved, and you are making good on the promise that students will be able to build on their scores. The grade at the end of the second marking period is also the grade for the semester. Do not average the semester final grades or the marking-period grades. The typical weight setting in an online gradebook for semester grades is likely 40–40–20, with each marking period at 40 percent and the midterm or final exam at 20 percent. But the weight can be set at 100 to prevent averaging. It can also be set at 80–20, to allow for a formal exam. Even for a teacher like me who is not especially tech-savvy, the options to support a student-centered approach to evaluation are already in the software. Once you enter the learning goals in the system and students understand what you expect, you'll spend much less time on bookkeeping and much more time conferring with students and responding to their work.

In their course evaluations, my students responded positively to all major components of the student-centered approach: emphasis on collaboration, individualized tasks and projects, shared learning goals, and student-teacher evaluation partnerships. They worked hard, understood what they accomplished, and were justly proud. Although the impact is huge, the shift in focus from good *grades* to good *learning* can be achieved with small, practical changes: the gradebook becomes a log of student work, student-teacher conferences and evaluation of progress toward achievement of course learning goals replace assignment grades, and a traditional exam verifies student-centered evaluation. And it can all happen in a traditional school with a longstanding commitment to averaged grades!

In his conclusion to *Transforming Classroom Grading*, Marzano (2000) writes, "Individual teachers, schools, and districts stand poised for action; they are ready for change. What is required now is for some members of that group to take the lead—to be the vanguard" (p. 122). Taking a student-centered approach requires stepping out of your comfort zone, but the reward for doing so is twofold. What you believe students need and what is actually going on in your classroom converge, giving you a sense of accomplishment and peace, and the students, no longer worried about grades, are free to engage deeply in learning. After a couple of years, even elementary students have the opportunity to observe many teachers, and students of all ages learn to read us well. They know whether or not we believe in what we're doing and what we're asking them to do. Taking a student-centered approach might not work perfectly at first, but when you know you're doing what's best for students, each step you and your students take away from the deeply flawed tradition of averaged grades will give you more freedom to deeply engage in teaching *and* learning.

I'll end this chapter with the conclusion a student named Quincy DeYoung wrote for her portfolio about what it's like to learn without the pressure of averaged grades. Her words are used here with her permission.

> *I used to write for other people. I used to write for the grade. It's sad to say but I did it often; my writing had become such a constricted and construed mess from staying within the confines of what I believed to be an A. It was not me; it was an attempt to please. No stream of consciousness because it's not grammatical?*
>
> *OK.*
>
> *Times New Roman, typed, 12-point font, no exceptions?*
>
> *OK.*
>
> *This year, however, has been different. This year I've seen writing treated as artwork, pieces of prose treated as masterpieces; it's as if students expressing their innermost thoughts upon paper is too valuable a thing to have a letter stamped upon it. . . . This year my writing skills have been honed, not labeled. I have been given suggestions for my writing, and written feedback to strengthen my weak points. Instead of fearing the rejection associated with a B–, I have stepped off the precipice and taken risks. From daily read arounds to essential-question workshops, I've learned to step out of my comfort zone and voice topics that speak to me.*

In the next chapter, we'll close things out with the sixth and final student-centered teaching practice: communicate with the school community. Although you might be trying this approach in isolation in your own classroom, it's also important to inform colleagues, administrators, and parents. I offer tips for doing so.

Next Steps for Meeting Individual Needs in the Evaluation Process

The following tool details some steps you can take to experiment with the evaluation process in your classroom. For each step, note the date you tried it and reflect on how it went: What did you do? How did it go? What would you change? What's next? There are spaces available at the end for you to plan additional steps you can take toward a student-centered approach to teaching.

Next Steps Tried	Date Tried	Reflection
Do a practice run with your school's progress-reporting system to confirm you can enter scores for progress toward learning goals instead of averaged grades.		
Decide on the source you will use for learning goals for your students: standardized test criteria, state or national standards, local curriculum documents, and so on.		
Select a doable number of learning goals for your students. Keep in mind, achieving a learning goal should require multiple skills students can demonstrate in a variety of subject areas.		
Decide what traditional assessment you will use to confirm your students' scores on learning goals are accurate.		

CHAPTER 6

Communicate With the School Community

Teachers who want to embark on a student-centered approach may encounter resistance arising from the misconceptions of administrators, colleagues, parents, or community members. One such misconception is that anecdotal evidence a teacher derives from direct observation of students is less valuable than quantifiable data from grades, test scores, student-conduct referrals, graduation rates, and so on. In fact, teachers are professionals who administrators, colleagues, parents, and community members can and should trust to observe, record, analyze, and express significant information about what goes on in the classroom—information that could have a major impact on the quality and efficacy of education if and when policy decisions take it into account.

A second misconception is that student-centered instruction is a feel-good approach that lacks academic rigor. But shifting the focus of a classroom from what the teacher is teaching to what the students are learning, to paraphrase Moffett and Wagner (1992), actually makes school harder and more fun—not only for the students, which is of course our focus, but for teachers as well. Larry Ferlazzo (2015), a high school teacher and author who has taken a particular interest in student motivation, confirms this assertation. Based on review of recent studies by researchers such as Carol Dweck and her colleagues at Stanford University and his own observations as a classroom teacher working with diverse groups of students, Ferlazzo (2015) identifies four qualities of the school experience that can help students motivate themselves: (1) autonomy, (2) competence, (3) relatedness, and (4) relevance. The research has shown that when students feel that they can trust their teachers to support their learning and that they belong in the classroom, they develop the positive mindset that allows them to work harder, overcome obstacles and setbacks, and feel optimistic about their progress and potential. This sense of trust and belonging is fortified by honest feedback from the teacher that is delivered with encouragement to persist. Praise must be earned, but teachers can be generous with encouragement to press on.

In a student-centered classroom, the focus is not just on academic success but on the well-being of the whole individual. Instead of doing things the way they have always been done, you can look for approaches and strategies that offer students the respect and support they need to fully engage in and enjoy learning. If you are concerned that some school community members may question or even object to your student-centered teaching practices, it can be tempting to close the classroom door and keep those practices to yourself. But sharing the student-centered approach with others is important and constitutes the sixth student-centered teaching practice: communicate with the school community. Sharing what you're doing and why you're doing it pushes you to articulate your practices and the reasons for them, and gets the word out that there are, indeed, alternatives to traditional methods for those who might have just started thinking along such lines. Your efforts will mainly focus on communicating with colleagues, administrators, and parents; the following sections offer further detail on each of these.

Communication With Colleagues

While it's unlikely other teachers will oppose your desire to take a student-centered approach, you may have to deal with lack of interest instead. In the following sections, I offer some strategies for overcoming this barrier.

Cast a Wide Net for Support

Teachers, by and large, like doing things the way they've always been done and don't want to change a culture that allows them to make up their own grading policies. But support doesn't have to be from the classroom next door. To provide the encouragement you need and deserve, there may be a colleague at another grade level, in another subject area, or in another building who is interested in a student-centered approach. Even though the teaching assignments are different, colleagues who share your interest in creating a student-centered classroom will lend a sympathetic ear when things don't go as you hoped. And, perhaps, they can offer a suggestion or tell a story from their own experience that will help. Students need a combination of honest feedback and encouragement, and so do teachers.

I found high school colleagues who were not only interested but also actively engaged in student-centered teaching in graphic arts, computer science, and physical education. And I also found colleagues in other buildings—middle schools and elementary schools—who welcomed my interest and shared their experience taking a student-centered approach with elementary and middle school students. Support is available online as well. There are thriving communities on Twitter and other social media; try searching #studentcentered and #edchat to begin.

Join a Cross-Grade or Interdisciplinary Team

In addition to personal support, I recommend that you seek established professional support by joining a school improvement council or participating in a district program. There's a lot to learn by volunteering for cross-grade or interdisciplinary teams that are looking at a specific subject area through a K–12 lens or conducting an interdisciplinary study of progress on a district initiative. For example, my district quality council launched an initiative to increase opportunities for students to be self-directed, and I joined a team charged with gathering and analyzing evidence to determine whether or not the initiative was having an impact. This was a big, complicated job, and it took months to organize and devise methods for gathering information in varied grades and subject areas so the teams could meaningfully compare and collate, and, finally, produce and present a report. I highly recommend that teachers seek out and get involved with initiatives like this. The months of interaction with team members develop camaraderie and a K–12 perspective, both of which provide indirect but valuable support for a teacher taking a student-centered approach.

You can also make your inbox a source of support by following newsletters and blogs. Some of my favorites are KQED's *MindShift* newsletter (www.kqed.org/mindshift), the George Lucas Educational Foundation's *Edutopia* newsletter (www.edutopia.org), and Alfie Kohn's thought-provoking blog entries (www.alfiekohn.org/blog). The *Teachers Going Gradeless* blog (www.teachersgoinggradeless.com) might be particularly helpful as you think about the role you want grades to play in your classroom. There are many more to choose from.

Take Advantage of Professional Development Opportunities

Although it took a while to realize it, one of the best pieces of advice I got while earning teacher certification was to take advantage of every opportunity to *get out of the classroom*. Time with students is precious, and it takes extra time to prepare to be out of the classroom, but the opportunity to be a student yourself at a stimulating conference is worth it. Funding for professional development tends to be limited and may be rationed or come with strings attached in the form of a requirement that you share what you learned at a department or faculty meeting. Do it anyway.

As a shy person looking back on a long career, my only regret is that I didn't step up sooner to offer workshops to my colleagues. Your first workshop may be a little rough around the edges, but I predict participants will appreciate your efforts even more when they see that being the presenter is a role that doesn't come easily for you—yet. And you will learn so much from the first workshop that the next one will go much more smoothly.

To prepare to make this happen at your school, start by observing others. When you attend a workshop or conference, give some attention to what the presenters do as well as what they're advising you to do. Notice what works for you and adapt those techniques for your own presentations. Your state may have a regional educational service that hosts workshops conducted by teachers for teachers. I attended and, eventually, presented at workshops hosted by two regional organizations: (1) Area Cooperative Education Services (ACES) and (2) Connecticut Educational Services

(CES). State branches of subject area organizations, in my case, Connecticut Council of Teachers of English, also host conferences that welcome teachers as participants and presenters. The National Writing Project offers summer programs open to all teachers and invitational programs that train teachers to develop and present workshops.

I devoted most of the summer of 1996 to an invitational program that pulled together teachers in K–12 and across content areas. It was worth it. The program instructors provided readings, modeled strategies, and organized our days together so there was plenty of time to give and get feedback. We met in the basement under the library at the University of Connecticut's Stamford campus. Even in the middle of a New England summer, the basement was so cold that we called it the walk-in freezer, but working together generated plenty of warmth. This poem was just one page in the thick binder of work I accumulated over the course of that summer.

Walk-In Freezer

A room furnished for many purposes:
fluorescent light, pianos pushed cock-eyed
into corners, ordered rows of squared seats
facing empty space, outlets that don't work.

It's cold. Our shoulders hunch inward, toes curl
in summer shoes. Numb fingers seek warmth, twirl
pencils, seeking friction, play with bangles.
Our knees seize up, bent at seated angles.

Sixteen fellows (most female), all ages,
use more paper than we planned, turn pages,
filled. We speak, think, write. Ideas flicker:
our words are warm fronts, make their own weather.

In a room with no windows, clouds race past,
made of light and shadow patterns that last.

Some districts will request suggestions from teachers about district and building professional development programs. If that's your situation, make it known that you are interested in programs related to the student-centered classroom.

Communication With Administrators

Administrators must choose their battles carefully and often decide that challenging the teachers' autonomy to determine their own grading systems is not the hill they want to die on. Ironically, you may owe your freedom to try something new to the very autonomy that makes changing the school culture on grades so difficult.

In the schools where I taught, an administrator would only ask a teacher to provide plans for review if others raised concerns about the teacher's performance. But I know of schools where administrative review of teachers' plans is routine. Whatever your circumstance, it's important to keep the principal informed even if it's only a courtesy. The principals I worked with had an open-door policy, so it was easy to drop in for an informal meeting when they had a free moment. If your principal likes to keep things on a more formal basis, you might send a copy of your handout for parents with a note that just says you're trying an alternative approach to evaluation and will provide updates. You're not asking permission; you're simply giving the principal a heads-up that something a little different is going on in your classroom. If a colleague or parent does happen to speak to the principal about your student-centered approach, it will not come as a surprise. And I would guess that if you surveyed administrators about what they like least, it would be surprises. In a large school, there may also be an assistant principal involved in faculty support (as opposed to student discipline) you should also inform.

At the district level, I've worked with several assistant superintendents actively engaged in the workings of each school. It was important for them to have firsthand knowledge, be a familiar face, and provide support as well as direction. If you have the good fortune to be working with such an administrator, you might want to share what you're doing at the district level as well as the building level. When I applied for the James Moffett Memorial Award, it was Linda Gejda, assistant superintendent, who not only supported my application but picked up the tab for my travel to Orlando, Florida, in October of 2010 to receive the award. When I thanked her, she turned the thanks around and said, "Your work is making us look good" (L. Gejda, personal communication, October 2010).

Just keep in mind, of course, that administrators have plenty to do. When he was principal of Newtown High School and known as Chip Dumais rather than Dr. Dumais, I remember him saying how busy he was, that his time was not his own. He wished he could speak with students in the cafeteria, visit classrooms, meet with a group that wanted a skateboard park, but he knew he would inevitably end up trapped in his office dealing with various issues as they came up. He and other administrators I've worked with liked teachers to deal with problems at the classroom level as much as possible. Taking a student-centered approach is likely to reduce the number of problems you need to solve, but sometimes students have issues just too big to resolve in the classroom, even with all the kindness, respect, and support you can muster. On such occasions, you'll be especially glad administrators know you and your teaching practices well.

If an administrator does challenge your plan to take a student-centered approach in your classroom, listen carefully to concerns, answer questions as best you can, offer information that supports the approach you want to take—perhaps a copy of this book will help!—and hope the administrator will begin to see the merit in what you want to try. If not, in that situation, I would address the concerns by modifying whatever aspect of the student-centered approach raised them, learn more, and try again later. Although change can come slowly, perceptions about what works in education do change with time, experience, and new evidence.

Communication With Parents

The idea that parents should be partners with teachers and administrators in their children's academic progress is nothing new, but these school-home partnerships don't always run smoothly. Sometimes parents expect too much, sometimes too little. Parental participation in school events tends to be high during the elementary years and gradually diminishes when the student goes to secondary school. Some parents might want very much to be more involved—volunteer in the classroom; attend parent-teacher-student association meetings; participate in fundraisers—but there are simply no hours and no energy left after long days or nights working multiple jobs, and the effort of communicating when the first language of the parent is not English is just too huge. Teachers and administrators may hear more often from parents who are unhappy than they do from parents who are satisfied with their children's school experience. Again, elementary school teachers tend to get more unconditional love than secondary school teachers. In my experience as a high school department chair, when a parent requests a meeting with a teacher, the teacher goes on the defensive, assuming (often correctly) the parent has a complaint and wants the teacher to resolve it by changing a grade. But I would argue that this kind of tension between parent and teacher is yet another form of fallout from traditional grading policies. Student-centered teaching practices in general, and student-centered evaluation in particular, promote strong school-home partnerships because taking this approach makes it so clear to parents how much the teacher cares about their children's success. In communicating with parents, it's important to expect and be open to questions and to become a familiar face by giving parents opportunities to see what students are doing in the classroom.

Expect Questions

When you first send information home about taking a student-centered approach, you might expect, as I did, plenty of emails and calls from parents expressing concern. Intellectually, parents understand their son or daughter is one among the many students each teacher serves, and they are usually satisfied as long as their child seems to like the teacher and the grades are good. Emotionally, parents believe their child deserves more, a feeling that intensifies when the teacher is doing something different. You can't help but wonder how you will defend the student-centered approach to a parent who doesn't understand why you aren't doing what every other teacher in the building is doing. It's so much more comfortable to just do what everyone else is doing. Going out on your own with something new makes you feel vulnerable. Just remind yourself that parental concerns arise from love and that it takes courage for a parent to communicate a concern to a teacher. In the initial handout, I wanted to let parents know I was trying something different yet refrain from second-guessing concerns. See figure 5.4 on page 106 for a short, simple explanation for parents of how student-centered evaluation works.

Parents worry that drawing attention to their child by expressing a concern will backfire in some way. And yet teachers do make mistakes, and, when this happens, we need to hear about it from those who bear the brunt: students and their parents. I predict you will receive only a few inquiries from parents. When these inquiries arrive, thank the parents for their interest, listen carefully to their concerns, provide additional detail, and hold your breath. In my experience, the parents' response was something along the lines of "Makes sense."

Become a Familiar Face

Your students are going to be doing some wonderful work that matters a great deal to them, so plan an event to showcase their hard work. The number of parents who are available for a special event during the school day seems to get smaller each year. It takes a fair amount of time and trouble to arrange an evening event for family and friends to see what your students have to present, but it's time well spent for everyone involved.

When you pick your date, check the school calendar, looking to avoid major school-wide events like plays and holiday concerts. In an elementary school, you might be able to arrange the furniture in your classroom in a way that allows room for everyone who might attend. In a secondary school, you will either need to find a larger space or schedule multiple events. If you are really lucky, your school will have a small lecture hall or theater. Sometimes an area of the cafeteria will have a stage. The library might have an area that works for this kind of event, or there might be a music rehearsal room that's just right. These tend to be popular spaces, so sign up early and make sure everyone who regularly uses the space knows about your event.

I recommend you schedule an event as early in the school year as possible while still giving your students time to become comfortable with their presentations and, of course, time to complete something they will want to show off. They might be ready in late October or early November, or you might want to wait until late January or early February. By all means, avoid the rush of field trips and events toward the end of the school year, and watch for blocks of time set aside for standardized testing.

The parent-teacher-student associations for the schools where I taught were serious about contributing to the quality of the school. You are probably already a person who has difficulty saying *no* when a chance to do something beneficial for your school and students comes along. And, of course, there's never enough time in a week for everything you need and want to do. All the same, if you have an opportunity to serve as a faculty representative with the parent-teacher-student association, consider accepting. It will give you a chance to get to know the parents who are doing behind-the-scenes work for the school, and it will give parents a chance to get to know you as a teacher they can count on. Some of these associations publish newsletters that welcome teacher contributions, so that's another way to become known and to share ideas and information about student-centered practices.

All six of the student-centered teaching practices this book offers have the potential not only to change your teaching paradigm but also to change your students' lives. Instead of simply producing work tailored to receive an A, students learn how to truly engage and think. Is there anything more important? Read on for some concluding thoughts and answers to some frequently asked questions about the student-centered approach.

Next Steps for Communicating With the School Community

The following tool details some steps you can take to experiment with communicating with the school community. For each step, note the date you tried it and reflect on how it went: What did you do? How did it go? What would you change? What's next? There are spaces available at the end for you to plan additional steps you can take toward a student-centered approach to teaching.

Next Steps Tried	Date Tried	Reflection
Do an internet search on student-centered teaching, and sign up for a relevant newsletter.		
Volunteer for a cross-grade or interdisciplinary team project.		
Find a colleague who will give you honest feedback on your plans and handouts.		
Join your school's parent-teacher-student association.		

The Student-Centered Classroom © 2021 Solution Tree Press • SolutionTree.com
Visit **go.SolutionTree.com/instruction** to download this free reproducible.

Epilogue
Conclusion

I had some wonderful teachers when I was a student in elementary and secondary school: Mrs. Harris, Mr. Cohen, Mrs. Binsacca, and Mr. Stulz. Each one of them found ways to support my learning and my development as an individual. Each one gave me a hard time when I didn't work to my full potential. And they all encouraged me to reach further than I thought I was able, both intellectually and creatively. I had them very much in mind when I became a teacher. Of course, taking on the responsibility of teaching others doesn't mean my own need for teachers ceased. If anything, the need to learn became more urgent.

Researchers, activists, and theorists such as Linda Darling-Hammond, Alfie Kohn, Walter Loban, Deborah Meier, James Moffett, Ted Sizer, and Betty Jane Wagner came to my rescue again and again: they influenced what happened in my classroom day to day and inspired me to persist in the process of creating a student-centered classroom. In turn, I encourage you to heed and amplify the people whose ideas you feel harmonize with the student-centered approach. Working together, sharing ideas, having the courage to try something different: you—as an educator, parent, community member—can make it possible to fulfill the promise of education in a democratic society. The stakes couldn't be higher, but I know that it can be done.

Like all change, shifting from traditional methods to a student-centered approach won't be easy at first. As a teacher, you'll have to think your way through practices that won't feel comfortable right away. As an administrator, you'll be figuring out how to evaluate what's going on in a classroom that seems to be running itself. As a parent, you'll need to be open to new ideas about grading and such. But if it starts to feel right, if students are responding positively—coming into the classroom with the light of expectation in their eyes, coming home excited about what they are learning—it will become easier until you reach a point of equilibrium where what you believe students should experience in school is actually what is happening.

Appendix
Frequently Asked Questions

This section gathers some of the most important ideas and passages from the book to provide quick answers to questions that I often hear.

Isn't a student-centered approach just for elementary school or for students who are disadvantaged?

All students, regardless of their grade level, learn better in an environment where all school staff respect, know, and support them.

How is a student-centered teaching approach different from a traditional teaching approach?

Instead of directing student learning, the teacher serves as a guide and mentor. The teacher must not only know the subject matter well but also know each student well. The teacher works with individuals and collaborative groups to identify areas of strength and need, and to personalize learning experiences that help each student build skill and confidence, instead of presenting one-size-fits-all lessons to an entire class. Student do not complete the same assignments in the same order; the teacher recognizes each student arrives in the classroom with a unique combination of prior knowledge and experience, so meeting individual needs requires flexible adaptation of tasks and sequence to meet students where they are. Lastly, the teacher does not grade assignments and report the average; the teacher provides timely, specific feedback on student work, and teacher and student work as partners to evaluate student progress toward achievement of learning goals.

Aren't averaged grades a more objective measure of student performance than student-teacher evaluations?

It might seem more objective to average grades on assignments, but just under the surface of this process is the potential for subjectivity and some built-in unfairness. Sometimes grades are more about student compliance or personality than the actual quality of the work. A few late or missing assignments can have a huge impact on the overall average. Similarly, an average that includes work done early in the marking period may not indicate how much the student actually learned. Students know a lot about how they are doing and are usually honest and accurate when they evaluate their progress. Teachers are professionals others can and should trust to observe, record, analyze, and express significant information about the progress each student is making and, more generally, what is and isn't working for students at a given age or academic level. This is information that could have a major impact on the quality and efficacy of education if and when policy decisions take it into account.

Isn't student-centered instruction just a feel-good approach that lacks academic rigor?

Shifting the classroom focus from what the teacher is teaching to what the students are learning, to paraphrase Moffett and Wagner (1992), makes school harder and more fun. Students work harder when they have some control over what and how they learn.

Does a student-centered approach mean teachers never grade students?

Students have grown increasingly concerned with amassing good grades, regardless of how little sleep they're getting or how much stress they have to manage on top of their packed schedules. The student-centered approach this book describes relieves students of some of that grade-related stress but doesn't do away with grades entirely. Students still receive grades necessary for transcripts and honor roll at the end of each marking period. But the emphasis shifts from teachers grading assignments to giving students feedback, and from teachers averaging students grades to assessing their progress toward achievement of learning goals.

If I don't enter a grade for each assignment, how will I keep track of what each student has done?

Once you stop grading individual assignments and focus instead on progress toward achievement of learning goals, students need to know you will still keep track of what they plan and complete—and that they will hear from you if you don't hear from them. You can keep a log of student work for this purpose.

What's the most important difference between traditional grading methods and the student-centered approach?

Traditional grading asks students, parents, counselors, and college admission offices to *infer* progress toward achievement of learning goals from assignment grades. But assignment grades are an intermediate step in the process of reporting student progress. The student-centered approach includes the teacher's detailed, timely feedback on student work in progress, but teachers do not grade individual assignments. The focus is directly on student progress toward achievement of learning goals, so students, parents, counselors, and college admission offices know exactly how each student is doing rather than having to infer progress from assignment grade averages.

Isn't collaboration just a time-out for the teacher and a free pass for students to socialize?

In a student-centered classroom, much of the important work occurs in groups. This approach invites students to work collaboratively to make progress toward achievement of learning goals. Students do not compete with one another to experience success. As Kohn (2019b) notes, "Indeed, a surprisingly consistent body of social science evidence shows that competition tends to hold us back from doing our best—particularly in comparison with cooperation, in which people work with, not against, each other."

How do I make sure students are actually getting work done in collaborative groups?

For student *collaboration* not to collapse into student *socialization*, it's important to plan ahead for group composition, task directions, and evaluation criteria. And it's also important to specifically include *interaction* in the course learning goals. This sends a clear message: interaction is important and progress toward achievement of essential interaction skills is part of the work each student is responsible for. The teacher should actively monitor student groups, both to troubleshoot and to comment when students do their jobs well. In the larger world of college and careers, having the ability to interact effectively with others that results from well-organized, sustained group work is highly portable and has the potential to open doors.

What is the purpose of a peer-conference group?

Peer-conference groups provide feedback on student work in progress. Peer-conference groups are important not just for the feedback but also for exposure to others' ideas, organizational strategies, stylistic devices, uses of humor, and so on. The work in progress could be a plan for a science experiment, a survey of student preferences regarding after-school programs, a diagram of a mathematics problem, an idea for a drawing, the lyrics for a song, and an infinite number of other possibilities.

What does it look like to share authority with students?

It's central to a student-centered approach to respect what students know about their strengths and needs, offer students topic choices, and make students partners in project design. When students have genuine opportunities to make choices and voice their opinions, the potential for their perceptions and insights to take the teacher by surprise increases. It feels a little awkward to respond to a student's idea by admitting, "I never thought of that," or "That's not the way I see it," instead of saying, "That's not correct," but it's thrilling to see students think for themselves.

Isn't classroom management a problem when teachers share authority with students?

As your classroom becomes student centered, I predict if management is an issue for you, it won't be any longer. Each student has a unique history, perspective, strengths, and needs. When you take the time to learn their stories, students feel known and trusted to want to learn. They will show you in so many ways they are ready to move forward with their learning and their lives.

Why is there so much focus on communication skills in a student-centered classroom?

Doing a good job on units of study and scoring well on standardized tests is not enough. Becoming ready to take an active role in the classroom and in the larger world requires solid communication skills and the confidence to put them to work. Across grade levels and content areas, students need positive experiences as speakers and listeners, and they must be confident about the following.

- Their thoughts merit clear expression.
- They can engage and move an audience.
- They can gather information and generate new ideas.
- They can understand and appreciate the ideas of others.

How do I decide what learning goals to focus on?

The learning goals you select should already be familiar to students and parents. Any well-written set of both challenging and accessible goals will work. You can use learning goals from local curriculum documents, goals related to state-mandated tests, College Board goals, or national goals in subject areas such as English language arts and mathematics. For learning goals related to areas such as spoken language and collaboration that are typically not included in standardized tests, a source that focuses on education philosophy (rather than testing) might be helpful (for example, Great Schools Partnership [www.greatschoolspartnership.org] or Partnership for 21st Century Learning [https://battelleforkids.org/networks/p21]).

How do I evaluate each student's progress toward achievement of learning goals?

As you review each student's work, it's important to place more emphasis on major projects and more recent work than on small activities and work done early in the marking period. If there is an area where the student is having difficulty, you will be able to say, "Don't be afraid of a low score now. Your scores will build throughout the year, so a low score just lets us know what you need to work on."

What's the best way to collect student work over a period of time?

Because the teacher bases evaluation on evidence of progress in the work each student does over a period of time (rather than averaged grades on assignments), it's important to save the work in some form of folder. For elementary students, who might need help with organization, you can collect work in folders kept in the classroom, where both student and teacher have easy access. As students move on to secondary school, more responsibility can shift to them to manage a collection in a folder that will likely combine handwritten work and digital storage. The teacher can save projects students send electronically on a flash drive or on Google Drive (https://google.com/drive). This makes it easy for you to access each student's work at home as well as in the classroom.

How can I find time to meet with each student for an evaluation conference?

Use some of the time you save by not grading every assignment to meet with students. As students become comfortable with the process of evaluating their progress toward achievement of course learning goals, the time you'll need for conferences will lessen. With secondary students, you could conduct the last round of conferences via email.

How can I verify the accuracy of students' scores for progress toward achievement of learning goals?

Design a traditional, grade-appropriate, subject-area exam, and ask students to take the exam both to show how they're doing from a different perspective and to practice traditional test-taking skills. When you enter the scores in your online gradebook, you want to see most students' scores on this exam are within a few points of their average scores on learning goals. If there are more than a few instances of disparity between the student's exam score and average scores on learning goals, ask yourself some questions: "Did the exam accurately represent what students worked on in class? Was the exam written well enough so students were not lured into incorrect or incomplete responses by ambiguously worded questions and prompts? Did too much emphasis on affective skills and not enough on academic performance (or vice versa) skew students' learning goal scores?"

How do I tailor learning for individual students and adhere to the curriculum at the same time?

Taking a student-centered approach doesn't mean the curriculum goes out the window; it just means the opportunities students need to develop the knowledge and skills embedded in the curriculum are designed with the individual student in mind. Each task should generate work students care about and are willing to revise, perhaps multiple times, to get it just right. And students should be active partners in figuring out how to tailor each task so it will fit their specific interests, strengths, and needs.

Why is it necessary to be flexible about the sequence of tasks and projects?

There is no one right way to organize material for students. There are as many ways to organize material as there are students with individual strengths and needs. If a student or a group needs to let go of a project that just isn't working and try something new, flexible sequencing of tasks and projects makes this not only possible but also simple. For example, if a student comes from another school district and has already studied whatever is going on in the class, no problem. Once you make the shift from averaging grades to reporting progress toward achievement of learning goals, it doesn't matter if students might not complete exactly the same assignments or exactly the same number of assignments; the focus is on what each student is learning rather than how many assignments the student turns in.

What if I don't have the support of colleagues or administrators?

It's unlikely other teachers or administrators will oppose your desire to take a student-centered approach. Instead of a lack of support, you may have to deal with lack of interest. Teachers like doing things the way they've always been done, and many don't want to change a culture that allows them to make up their own grading policies. Administrators must choose their battles carefully, and often they decide challenging the teachers' autonomy to determine their own grading systems is not the hill they want to die on. Ironically, you may owe your freedom to try something new to the very autonomy that makes changing the school culture on grades so difficult.

Support doesn't have to be from the classroom next door or the principal's office to provide the encouragement you need and deserve. There may be a colleague at another grade level, in another subject area, or in another building who is interested in a student-centered approach. Request professional development opportunities related to the student-centered classroom. You can also make your inbox a source of support by signing up for newsletters and blogs. Some of my favorites are KQED's *MindShift* newsletter (www.kqed.org/mindshift), the George Lucas Educational Foundation's *Edutopia* newsletter (www.edutopia.org), and Alfie Kohn's thought-provoking blog entries (www.alfiekohn.org/blog). There are many more to choose from.

What if parents object to a student-centered approach?

Devote extra time and thought to the handouts you will distribute to parents the first time you decide to depart from averaging grades. You want it to be clear that you're trying something new and yet allay their concerns without too much second-guessing. Keep the explanation of your evaluation process short and clear. Parents tend to trust teachers to have their child's best interests at heart. When they can see their son or daughter really enjoying your class and clearly making progress, their response to a student-centered approach is likely to be "Makes sense."

References and Resources

Abbott, D. (2016, September). What brain regions control our language? And how do we know this? *The Conversation*. Accessed at https://theconversation.com/what-brain-regions-control-our-language-and-how-do-we-know-this-63318 on May 11, 2020.

Alper, C. (2018, August 17). *Embracing inquiry-based instruction*. Accessed at www.edutopia.org/article/embracing-inquiry-based-instruction on May 22, 2020.

Baeder, J. (Producer). (2016, September 5). *Principal center radio* [Audio podcast]. Accessed at www.podbean.com/ew/pb-siprd-db7c8f on May 8, 2020.

Berwick, C. (2019, March 28). How a literacy-first program revived a school. *Edutopia*. Accessed at www.edutopia.org/article/how-literacy-first-program-revived-school on May 7, 2020.

Boaler, J. (2019a, September 23). How collaboration unlocks learning and lessens student isolation. *MindShift*. Accessed at www.kqed.org/mindshift/54486/how-collaboration-unlocks-learning-and-lessens-student-isolation on April 29, 2020.

Boaler, J. (2019b). *Limitless mind: Learn, lead, and live without barriers*. New York: HarperOne.

Bradbury, R. (1953). *Fahrenheit 451*. New York: Ballantine Books.

Bransford, J. D., & Schwartz, D. L. (1999). Rethinking transfer: A simple proposal with multiple implications. In A. Iran-Nejad & P. D. Pearson (Eds.), *Review of research in education* (vol. 24, pp. 61–100). Washington, DC: American Educational Research Association.

Bridges, R. (1999). *Through my eyes*. New York: Scholastic Press.

Bullen, P. B. (2013). *How to choose a sample size (for the statistically challenged)*. Accessed at www.tools4dev.org/resources/how-to-choose-a-sample-size/ on May 6, 2020.

Cimpian, J. (2018, April 23). *How our education system undermines gender equity and why culture change—not policy—may be the solution*. Accessed at www.brookings.edu/blog/brown-center-chalkboard/2018/04/23/how-our-education-system-undermines-gender-equity/ on May 11, 2020.

Cleary, M. N. (2014, February 25). The wrong way to teach grammar. *The Atlantic.* Accessed at www.theatlantic.com/education/archive/2014/02/the-wrong-way-to-teach-grammar/284014 on May 11, 2020.

College Board. (n.d.). *AP English language and composition.* Accessed at https://apcentral.collegeboard.org/courses/ap-english-language-and-composition?course=ap-english-language-and-composition on January 3, 2020.

Curriculum Study Commission. (1992). Asilomar 42 is dedicated to Walter Loban. *Voices of California: Some regions of the mind* [Conference program]. San Francisco: Central California Council of Teachers of English.

Darling-Hammond, L., Flook, L., Cook-Harvey, C., Barron, B., & Osher, D. (2019). Implications for educational practice of the science of learning and development. *Applied Developmental Science.* Accessed at www.tandfonline.com/doi/full/10.1080/10888691.2018.1537791 on May 4, 2020.

Dewey, J. (1900). *The school and society: Being three lectures.* Chicago: University of Chicago Press.

Dewey, J. (1990). *The school and society; and, the child and the curriculum.* Chicago: University of Chicago Press.

Emily Dickinson Museum. (n.d.). *Emily Dickinson and the church.* Accessed at www.emilydickinsonmuseum.org/emily-dickinson/biography/special-topics/emily-dickinson-and-the-church/ on May 11, 2020.

Ferlazzo, L. (2015, September 14). Strategies for helping students motivate themselves. *Edutopia.* Accessed at www.edutopia.org/blog/strategies-helping-students-motivate-themselves-larry-ferlazzo on May 10, 2020.

Finney, K., & Giansante, L. (n.d.). *Writing with writers: Speechwriting.* Accessed at http://teacher.scholastic.com/writewit/speech/index.htm on 11 May 2020.

Frey, N., & Fisher, D. (2013). *Rigorous reading.* Thousand Oaks, CA: Corwin Literary.

Fudge, T. (2015, February 25). *Inductive vs. deductive writing.* Accessed at https://purdueglobalwriting.center/2015/02/25/inductive-vs-deductive-writing/ on May 6, 2020.

Gasoi, E., & Meier, D. (2018). To strengthen democracy, invest in our public schools. *American Educator.* Accessed at www.aft.org/ae/spring2018/gasoi_meier on January 3, 2020.

Ginsberg, A. (2001). *Selected poems 1947–1995.* New York: HarperCollins.

Gopnik, A. (2012, January 28). What's wrong with the teenage mind? *Wall Street Journal.* Accessed at www.wsj.com/articles/SB10001424052970203806504577181351486558984 on May 20, 2020.

Great Schools Staff. (2017, July 24). *Your fifth grader and math.* Accessed at www.greatschools.org/gk/articles/fifth-grade-math on January 3, 2020.

Heslov, G. (Producer), & Clooney, G. (Director). (2005). *Good night, and good luck* [Motion picture]. United States: Warner Independent Pictures.

Hopkins, A. (Producer), & Palcy, E. (Director). (1998). *Ruby Bridges* [Motion picture]. Burbank, CA: Walt Disney Television.

Jakicic, C. (2019, June 17). Do you have a "stop doing" list? *All Things Assessment.* Accessed at https://allthingsassessment.info/2019/06/17/a-stop-doing-list/ on May 15, 2020.

Johnson, D. (2018, April 30). What to feed wild deer. *Sciencing.* Accessed at https://sciencing.com/feed-wild-deer-5495043.html on February 24, 2020.

Kittle, P. (n.d.). *Elements of a reading workshop to increase stamina, fluency, and joy.* Accessed at https://pennykittle.net/uploads/images/PDFs/Workshop_Handouts/ReadingWorkshophandouts.pdf on May 7, 2020.

Kohn, A. (2019a, September 3). "Should grades be based on classwork?" And other questions we should stop asking. *Education Week.* Accessed at www.edweek.org/ew/articles/2019/09/04/should-grades-be-based-on-classwork-and.html on July 18, 2020.

Kohn, A. (2019b, June 15). Why can't everyone get A's? Excellence is not a zero sum game. *New York Times.* Accessed at www.nytimes.com/2019/06/15/opinion/sunday/schools-testing-ranking.html on January 3, 2020.

Korkki, P. (2014, March 12). *The science of older and wiser.* Accessed at www.nytimes.com/2014/03/13/business/retirementspecial/the-science-of-older-and-wiser.html on May 12, 2020.

Lamothe, M. (2017). *This is how we do it: One day in the lives of seven kids from around the world.* San Francisco: Chronicle Books.

Lee, H. Y., Jamieson, J. P., Miu, A. S., Josephs, R. A., & Yeager, D. S. (2018, July 10). An entity theory of intelligence predicts higher cortisol levels when high school grades are declining. *Child Development, 90*(6), e849–e867. Accessed at https://doi.org/10.1111/cdev.13116 on May 8, 2020.

Levinson, M. (2012, June 7). How do we help kids make better choices? Let them practice. *Edutopia.* Accessed at www.edutopia.org/blog/student-achievement-practice-matt-levinson on May 12, 2020.

Lindblom, K. (2009). From the editor. *English Journal, 99*(2), 11.

Loban, W. (1966, September). *The spoken word and the integrity of English instruction* (Study group paper no. 1). Accessed at https://files.eric.ed.gov/fulltext/ED082206.pdf on May 12, 2020.

Loban, W. (1976). *Language development: Kindergarten through grade twelve* (Research report no. 18). Urbana, IL: National Council of Teachers of English.

Loyola, S. W. (2016, September 9). In language classrooms, students should be talking. *Edutopia.* Accessed at www.edutopia.org/blog/in-language-classrooms-students-should-be-talking-sarah-wike-loyola on May 12, 2020.

Marion, S. (n.d.). *Following their lead: Some thoughts about student-led assessment.* Accessed at https://centerpointeducation.org/guest-post/following-their-lead-some-thoughts-about-student-led-assessment on May 13, 2020.

Marshall, F. (Producer), Buffet, J. (Producer), & Shriner, W. (Director). (2006). *Hoot* [Motion picture]. Burbank, CA: Warner Bros.

Martin, B. (2003, July). A writing assignment/A way of life. *English Journal*, *92*(6), 52–56.

Marzano, R. J. (2000). *Transforming classroom grading*. Alexandria, VA: Association for Supervision and Curriculum Development.

Marzano, R. J. (2013, May). Art and science of teaching / Targets, objectives, standards: How do they fit? *Educational Leadership*, *70*(8), 82–83. Accessed at www.ascd.org/publications/educational-leadership/may13/vol70/num08/Targets,-Objectives,-Standards@-How-Do-They-Fit%C2%A2.aspx on May 9, 2020.

Marzano, R. J. (2017). *The new art and science of teaching*. Bloomington, IN: Solution Tree Press.

Marzano, R. J. (2018). *Making classroom assessments reliable and valid*. Bloomington, IN: Solution Tree Press.

Marzano, R. J., Pickering, D. J., & Pollock, J. E. (2001). *Classroom instruction that works: Research-based strategies for increasing student achievement*. Alexandria, VA: Association for Supervision and Curriculum Development.

McCarthy, J. (2015, August 28). 3 ways to plan for diverse learners. *Edutopia*. Accessed at www.edutopia.org/blog/differentiated-instruction-ways-to-plan-john-mccarthy on May 9, 2020.

McKenna, B. (2014, June 17). *New research shows effectiveness of student-centered learning in closing the opportunity gap*. Accessed at https://ed.stanford.edu/news/new-research-shows-effectiveness-student-centered-learning-closing-opportunity-gap on April 27, 2020.

Miller, J. J. (2013). A better grading system: Standards-based, student-centered assessment. *English Journal*, *103*(1), 111–118.

Moffett, J. (1994). *The universal schoolhouse: Spiritual awakening through education*. San Francisco: Jossey-Bass.

Moffett, J., & Wagner, B. J. (1992). *Student-centered language arts, K–12.* (4th ed.). Portsmouth, NH: Boynton/Cook.

Morris, J. (Producer), & Stanton, A. (Director). (2008). *WALL-E* [Motion picture]. Burbank, CA: Pixar Animation Studios for Walt Disney Pictures.

Morrison, T. (1987). *Beloved*. New York: Knopf.

Mould, S. (2018). *The bacteria book: The big world of really tiny microbes*. New York: DK Children.

Muñoz, M. A., & Guskey, T. R. (2015). Standards-based grading and reporting will improve education. *Phi Delta Kappan*, *96*(7), 64–68. Accessed at http://tguskey.com/wp-content/uploads/Grading-7-Standards-Based-Grading-Will-Improve-Education.pdf on May 8, 2020.

National Commission on Excellence in Education. (1983, April). *A nation at risk: The imperative for educational reform.* Washington, DC: Government Printing Office. Accessed at https://edreform.com/wp-content/uploads/2013/02/A_Nation_At_Risk_1983.pdf on February 24, 2020.

National Scientific Council on the Developing Child. (2014). *Excessive stress disrupts the architecture of the developing brain.* Accessed at https://developingchild.harvard.edu/wp-content/uploads/2005/05/Stress_Disrupts_Architecture_Developing_Brain-1.pdf on May 8, 2020.

Nelson, R. (2009). *Deer.* Minneapolis, MN: Lerner.

O'Brien, T. (1990). *The things they carried: A work of fiction.* Boston: Houghton Mifflin Harcourt.

Pandolpho, B. (2018, May 30). 4 ways to help student writers improve. *Edutopia.* Accessed at www.edutopia.org/article/4-ways-help-student-writers-improve on May 12, 2020.

Pandolpho, B. (2020). *I'm listening: How teacher-student relationships improve reading, writing, speaking, and listening.* Bloomington, IN: Solution Tree Press.

Partnership for 21st Century Learning. (2019). *Framework for 21st century learning definitions.* Accessed at http://static.battelleforkids.org/documents/p21/P21_Framework_Definitions BFK.pdf on February 19, 2020.

Poetry Out Loud. (n.d.). *Tips on reciting.* Accessed at www.poetryoutloud.org/competing/tips-on-reciting on January 3, 2020.

Quist, A., & Gregory, R. (2019, May 2). *Teaching decision-making skills in the classroom.* Accessed at www.arithmeticofcompassion.org/blog/2019/5/1/teaching-decision-making-skills-in-the-classroom on May 1, 2020.

Reading Rockets. (n.d.). *Choral reading.* Accessed at www.readingrockets.org/strategies/choral_reading on May 12, 2020.

Rebora, A. (2016, June 20). Remodeling the workshop: Lucy Calkins on writing instruction today. *Education Week.* Accessed at www.edweek.org/tm/articles/2016/06/20/remodeling-the-workshop-lucy-calkins-on-writing.html on May 6, 2020.

Reeves, D. B. (2008). Leading to change / Effective grading practices. *Educational Leadership, 65*(5), 85–87. Accessed at www.ascd.org/publications/educational-leadership/feb08/vol65/num05/Effective-Grading-Practices.aspx on January 3, 2020.

Reeves, D. B. (2015). *Inspiring creativity and innovation in K–12.* Bloomington, IN: Solution Tree Press.

Reeves, D. B. (2017, November 2). *Busting myths about grading.* Accessed at www.illuminateed.com/blog/2017/11/busting-myths-about-grading/ on May 12, 2020.

Reeves, D. B., & Reeves, B. (2017). *The myth of the muse: Supporting virtues that inspire creativity.* Bloomington, IN: Solution Tree Press.

Regan, M. (2013, November 22). 3 strategies to promote independent thinking in classrooms. *Edutopia.* Accessed at www.edutopia.org/blog/3-strategies-promote-independent-thinking-margaret-regan on May 13, 2020.

Rockwell, N. (1964). *The problem we all live with* [Oil on canvas]. Norman Rockwell Museum, Stockbridge, MA.

Sammons, L. R. (2017, May 26). *Adapting instruction through differentiation.* Accessed at www.solutiontree.com/blog/adapting-instruction-through-differentiation/ on May 9, 2020.

Sawchuk, S. (2016, June 20). Is the five paragraph essay history? *Education Week.* Accessed at www.edweek.org/tm/articles/2016/06/20/is-the-five-paragraph-essay-history.html on May 6, 2020.

Schimmer, T. (2016). *Grading from the inside out: Bringing accuracy to student assessment through a standards-based mindset.* Bloomington, IN: Solution Tree Press.

School Redesign Network. (2008). *What is performance-based assessment?* Accessed at https://edpolicy.stanford.edu/sites/default/files/events/materials/2011-06-linked-learning-performance-based-assessment.pdf on May 12, 2020.

Schrock, K. (2018). *Research and style manual: Works cited for grades 1–6.* Accessed at www.schrockguide.net/uploads/3/9/2/2/392267/workscited_1_6.pdf on May 5, 2020.

Silver, H. F., Strong, R. W., & Perini, M. J. (2000). *So each may learn.* Alexandria, VA: Association for Supervision and Curriculum Development.

Sizer, T. R. (1984). *Horace's compromise: The dilemma of the American high school.* Boston: Houghton Mifflin.

Steinbeck, J. (1945). *Cannery row.* New York: Viking Press.

Sternberg, R. J. (n.d.). *Balance theory of wisdom.* Accessed at www.robertjsternberg.com/wisdom on May 14, 2020.

Sternberg, R. J. (2008). Assessing what matters. *Educational Leadership, 65*(4), 20–26.

Stiggins, R. (2017). *The perfect assessment system.* Alexandria, VA: Association for Supervision and Curriculum Development.

Stiggins, R., & Chappuis, J. (2006). What a difference a word makes: Assessment FOR learning rather than assessment OF learning helps students succeed. *Journal of Staff Development, 27*(1), 10–14. Accessed at www.jaymctighe.com/wp-content/uploads/2011/04/Assessment-for-Learning.pdf on May 8, 2020.

Stuart, D. (2017, May 9). *The pyramid of writing priorities.* Accessed at https://davestuartjr.com/pyramid-writing-priorities/ on May 5, 2020.

Swift, J. (2019). *A modest proposal.* Accessed at www.gutenberg.org/files/1080/1080-h/1080-h.htm on June 17, 2020.

Thompson-Grove, G. (n.d.). *Text-based seminar guidelines.* Accessed at http://adw.org/wp-content/uploads/2014/09/Text-Based-Seminar-Protocol.pdf on January 3, 2020.

Tomlinson, C. (2017). *How to differentiate instruction in academically diverse classrooms* (3rd ed.). Alexandria, VA: Association for Supervision and Curriculum Development.

Units of Study. (n.d.). *The predictable 5-part workshop framework*. Accessed at http://unitsofstudy.com/framework on May 7, 2020.

University of Queensland. (n.d.). *Three minute thesis: About*. Accessed at https://threeminutethesis.uq.edu.au/about on May 3, 2020.

Usable Knowledge. (2017, September 7). *The value of listening*. Accessed at www.gse.harvard.edu/news/uk/17/09/value-listening on May 10, 2020.

Waterford.org. (2020, March 3). *The value of listening in the classroom: How to teach your students active listening*. Accessed at www.waterford.org/education/active-listening-in-the-classroom/ on May 3, 2020.

Werner, D. (2013). *Acts of kindness: Narrative writing*. Accessed at https://purdueglobalwriting.center/2013/12/13/actsofkindnessnarrativewriting/ on May 6, 2020.

Whitman, W. (1995). *Civil War poetry and prose*. New York: Dover.

Wiggins, G., & McTighe, J. (2005). *Understanding by design* (Expanded 2nd ed.). Alexandria, VA: Association for Supervision and Curriculum Development.

Wiley, J., & Hulsey, C. (n.d.). *Living on the edge: How deer survive winter*. Accessed at www.maine.gov/ifw/docs/deer_yards.pdf on May 21, 2020.

Wolfe, T. (1973). *The new journalism*. New York: Harper & Row.

Wormeli, R. (2006). *Fair isn't always equal: Assessing and grading in the differentiated classroom*. Portland, ME: Stenhouse.

Index

A

ACES. *See* Area Cooperative Educational Services
adapting, 35
administrators
    communicating with, 122–124
    lack of support from, 136–137
Allan, S., 101
Alper, C., 94–96
alternative schools, 5–6
alternatives, 35
American Psychological Association, 65
anecdotal records, 100–101, 111–112
    sample, 111
Area Cooperative Educational Services (ACES), 121
As for all, 1–1
assessment
    criterion-referenced, 8–9
    electronic gradebook example, 114
    flexible, 49–50
    flexible sequencing, 99–105
    formative, 96, 100
    learning goal descriptions, 113
    next steps, 118
    performance-based, 8–9
    problems with traditional grading systems, 89–94
    sample anecdotal record, 111
    sample rubric for essay questions, 115
    sample student progress logs, 110–111
    self, 100–101, 107
    shared evaluation of student progress, 105–117
    student work log example, 104
    student-centered approach, 94–97
    teacher's evaluation process explanation, 106
    timely, specific feedback, 97–99
    traditional gradebook example, 103
The Atlantic, 65
attitude surveys, 23
audience experience, 57
autonomy, 119
autotelic activities, 28
averaged grades, 132

B

background information, 82–83
Baeder, J., 98
"Balance Theory of Wisdom" (Sternberg), 31
Bard College
    Institute for Thinking and Writing, 80
Barron, B., 66
"Beat! Beat! Drums!" (Whitman), 83
Beato, K., 80
bell curve, 1
Beloved (Morrison), 7
Berwick, C., 81
Boaler, J., 17–18
Bradbury, R., 12
brainstorming, 29, 49, 58, 69

Bransford, J. D., 66
break it down, 82–83
Bullen, P. B., 74
bullying, 36–37
bumper sticker, 82–83
"Busting Myths About Grading" (Reeves), 92–93

C

Calkins, L., 67
Cannery Row (Steinbeck), 1–2
Carstensen, L. L., 29, 31
cause–effect text structure, 67
CCCTE. *See* Central California Council of Teachers of English
Central California Council of Teachers of English (CCCTE), 40
CES. *See* Connecticut Educational Services
Chicago Manuel of Style, 65
choral reading, 44–48
    defined, 44
    performance guidelines, 46–47
chronology text structure, 67
citing sources, 65–66
Classroom Instruction That Works (Marzano et al.), 53
Clayton, V., 30–31
Cleary, M. N., 65–66
Clooney, G., 12
Coalition of Essential Schools, 105
collaboration groups, 17–19
    help with decision making, 36–37
    reflection questions, 19
    romantic interests, 18
collaborative learning. *See* group work
collaborative reading, 100
    workshop, 81–82
colleagues
    cross-grade or interdisciplinary teams, 120–121
    finding support, 120
    lack of support from, 136–137
    professional development opportunities, 121–123
College Board, 99
communicating
    focus on, 134
    next steps, 127
    with administrators, 123–124
    with colleagues, 120–123
    with parents, 124–126
    with the school community, 9, 119–120
compare–contrast text structure, 67
competence, 119
Connecticut Council of Teachers of English, 122
Connecticut Educational Services (CES), 121
consequences, 35
Cook-Harvey, C., 66
Cooperative Educational Services, Fairfield Country, Conn., 91
criterion-referenced assessment, 8–9
cross-grade teams, 120–121, 127
Csikszentmihalyi, M., 28, 31
cultural norms, 12
Curriculum Study Committee, 40

D

Darling-Hammond, L., 3, 66, 129
decision making
    low-risk, 34–35
    practicing, 36
    six steps, 35
deduction, 68
Delta School District (British Columbia), 35
description text structure, 67
Dewey, J., 7, 105
DeYoung, Q., 117
Dickenson, E., 36
"Do You Have a 'Stop Doing' List?" (Jakicic), 97
Dumais, C., 91, 123
Dweck, C., 119

E

Education Week, 4, 67
Educational Leadership, 30
Edutopia newsletter (George Lucas Educational Foundation), 121, 137
electronic gradebooks, 112–116
    sample, 114
Emerson, R. W., 11

encouragement vs. praise, 119
encouraging academic success
    individualization, 11, 24
    integration with student interests, 11–13
    interaction among students, 11, 13–24
    next steps, 25
enduring tasks, 99
English Journal, 31
evaluation conferences, 135

F

factory model, 7–8
Fahrenheit 451 (Bradbury), 12
Fair Isn't Always Equal (Wormeli), 94
feedback, 131
    form, 56
    formative assessment, 100
    peer-conference groups, 19–20
    short speeches, 56–57
    soliciting, 127
    surveys, 74, 76
    timely and specific, 97–99
Ferlazzo, L., 119
field research, 68–70
    interviews, 70–72
    narrative devices, 75–77
    surveys, 72–75
finding support, 120, 136-137
    online, 120, 137
Fischer, L., 68
Fisher, D., 62
flexible sequencing, 96, 99–105, 131, 136
Flook, L., 66
formative assessment, 96, 100
formatting, 66–68
framing, 35
frequently asked questions, 131–137
Frey, N., 61

G

Gasoi, E., 27
Gejda, L., 123
gender expectations, 12
George Lucas Educational Foundation, 121, 137
Gibbons, G., 65
Ginsberg, A., 12
Good Night, and Good Luck (Heslov & Clooney), 12
Google Drive, 110, 135
Gopnik, A., 36
Grading From the Inside Out (Schimmer), 98
Gregory, R., 34–35
group talk, 41–43
group work, 11, 13–15, 33, 100–101
    collaboration groups, 17–19
    goals, 17
    peer-conference groups, 15–16, 19–24
    vs. socialization, 15, 133
guidelines
    essay assignment, 29
    interviewing, 72–73
    letters to the editor, 78–79
    peer-conference groups, 20–21
    role playing, 44
    surveys, 74–75
    vs. directions, 29
Guskey, T. R., 92, 98

H

Hall, R. B., 3–4, 82
Harvard University
    National Scientific Council on the Developing Child, 90
    Usable Knowledge, 48
Henss, M., 45–48
Heslov, G., 12
Hopkins, A., 3
Horace's Compromise (Sizer), 8
How to Differentiate Instruction in Academically Diverse Classrooms (Tomlinson), 101
"Howl" (Ginsburg), 12
Humpty Dumpty, 49

I

"I Hear America Singing" (Whitman), 82–83
"I Hear It Was Charged Against Me" (Whitman), 83
I'm Listening (Pandolpho), 61
imaginative freedom, 27, 31–34
imagine talk, 43

independent thinking, 27–31
individualization, 11, 24
    in assessment, 89–118
induction, 68
integrity, 27, 34–37
interdisciplinary teams, 120–121, 127
interviewing, 70–72
    guidelines, 72–73

J

Jakicic, C., 97
James Moffett Classroom Research Award, 123

K

Kohn, A., 2–4, 7, 121, 129, 133, 137
KQED, 121, 137

L

Lamothe, M., 63
leading questions, 73
leaps of imagination. *See* imaginative freedom
learning goals, 112, 115
    assessment of progress, 99–105
    content-specific, 97
    deciding what to focus on, 134–136
    evaluating progress, 135
    full descriptions, 113
    investment in, 69
    samples, 16–17
learning styles, 5
letters to the editor
    guidelines, 78–79
likely conditions, 3, 8
Limitless Mind (Boaler), 17
Lindblom, K., 31, 34
listening, 9
    occasional papers, 48–52
    short speeches, 52–57
    through writing and speaking, 48
Loban, W., 40, 129
Loyola, S. W., 40–41

M

Making Classroom Assessments Reliable and Valid (Marzano), 98
making space for speaking and listening, 39–40
    enhanced listening through writing and speaking, 48–57
    next steps, 58–59
    speech to facilitate thought, 40–48
Marion, S., 105
Marks, A., 94
Martha's Vineyard Master Teaching Institute, 28
Martin, B., 48–49
Marzano, R. J., 53, 97–99, 116
McCarthy, J., 101
McKenna, B., 2
McTighe, J., 24
Meier, D., 7, 27, 129
Meier, J., 44
micro-revision, 54
Mind/Shift newsletter (KQED), 121, 137
modeling, 62
Modern Language Association, 65
Moffett, J., 7, 13, 18, 27, 61, 94–96, 119, 129, 132
Monarch Butterflies (Gibbons), 65
Morrison, T., 7
Munoz, M. A., 98
The Myth of the Muse (Reeves & Reeves), 32

N

narrative devices, 75–77
narrative guidelines, 70–71
A Nation at Risk (National Commission on Excellence in Education), 7
National Center for the Improvement of Educational Assessment, 105
National Commission on Excellence in Education, 7
National Novel Writing Month, 49
National School Reform Faculty, 84
National Staff Development Council, 95–96
National Writing Project, 122
The New Art and Science of Teaching (Marzano), 98
The New Journalism (Wolfe), 75
Newtown (Conn.) High School, 68, 90–91, 94, 123

next steps
    encouraging academic success, 25
    reading and writing, 88
    speaking and listening, 58–59
    student-centered assessment, 118
    supporting personal growth, 38
Northwest Regional Educational Laboratory Centers for Classroom Assessment and Performance Assessment, 96
note to self, 82

O

O'Brien, T., 28–29, 45
objectives, 35
occasional papers, 48–49
    flexible dates and assessment, 49–50
    guidelines, 50
    Hallmark Factory, 51
    staying on topic, 52
    taking risks, 52
    writing with students, 51
online grading systems, 116
Osher, D., 66

P

paired interviews, 42–43
    worksheet, 42
Palcy, E., 3
Pandolpho, B., 61
parents
    become a familiar face, 125–126
    communicating with, 124
    expect questions, 124–125
    resistance, 137
parent-teacher-student associations, 125–127
Partnership for 21st Century Learning, 99
peer-conference groups, 15–16, 19–24
    demonstrating a bad one, 22
    guidelines, 20–21
    purpose, 133–134
Perfect Assessment System THE (Stiggins), 96
performance-based assessment, 8–9
personal growth. *See* supporting personal growth
philosophies of instruction, 102
Pickering, D. J., 53

Poetry Out Loud, 45
Pollock, J. E., 53
PostSecret, 49
preferences, 35
presentation sequence, 56–57
Principal's Corner Radio, 98
The Problem We All Live With (Rockwell), 3, 82
problem–solution text structure, 67
process writing, 63–64
professional development, 121–122
project-based learning. *See* group work
Proteus Project (Fischer), 68
provisional writing, 62–63
Purdue University
    Global Writing Center, 68

Q

Quaker read, 82, 84
Quist, A., 34–35

R

reading, 9
    background information, 82–83
    break it down, 82–83
    bumper sticker, 82–83
    collaborative reading workshop, 81–82
    deepening understanding with, 61–62
    illuminating the process of, 80–81
    next steps, 88
    note to self, 82
    Quaker read, 82, 84
    response to prompts, 82–83
    shift in perspective, 82
    text-based discussions, 84–87
Readingrockets.org, 44
realistic dialogue, 76
recursive approach, 81–82
Reeves, B., 32–33
Reeves, D. B., 32–33, 91–93
Regan, M., 28
relatedness, 119
relevance, 5, 119
    student interests, 11–13
researched narratives
    format, 66–68

process writing, 63–64
provisional writing, 62–63
samples, 64
sources, 65–66
resources, 121, 136–137
response to prompts, 82–83
Rigorous Reading (Frey & Fisher), 62
Rockwell, N., 3, 82
role playing, 43–44
    guidelines, 44
rubric for essay questions, 115
Ruby Bridges (Hopkins & Palcy), 3

S

Sammons, L. R., 101–102
sample curriculum goals, 14
sample traditional gradebook, 103
Sawchuk, S., 68
scene-by-scene construction, 76
Schimmer, T., 98
Scholastic Assessment Test, 31
The School and Society (Dewey), 7
Schrock, K., 65
Schwartz, D. L., 66
self-assessment, 96, 101, 115
    charts, 100, 107
semester killer, 92
shared evaluation of student progress, 105–117
sharing authority, 134
shift in perspective, 82
short speeches, 52–54
    audience experience, 57
    micro-revision, 54
    presentation sequence and feedback, 56–57
    sample scripts, 55–56
    timing, 54
Silver, H. F., 1–2
Sizer, T. R., 7–8, 105, 129
So Each May Learn (Silver et al.), 1
Society for Research in Child Development (SRCD), 90
Sorde, A., 80
speaking, 9
    choral reading, 44–48
    group talk, 41–43
    making space for, 39–40
    role playing, 43–44
    short speeches, 52–57
    to facilitate thought, 40–41
"The Spoken Word and the Integrity of English Instruction" (Loban), 40
SRCD. *See* Society for Research in Child Development
"Standards-Based Grading Will Improve Education" (Munoz & Guskey), 98
Stanford University, 119
    Center for Opportunity Policy in Education (SCOPE), 3
    Center on Longevity, 30
    School Redesign Network, 8–9
status life details, 77
Steinbeck, J., 1–2
Sternberg, R. J., 30–31
Stiggins, R., 96
stress, 90–91
Stuart, D., 62–64
student interests, 11–13
student progress log, 109, 132
student work log, 103–105
Student-Centered Language Arts, K–12 (Moffett & Wagner), 18, 27
Student-centered learning, 3, 6–8, 10
    assessment, 8–9, 89–118
    at all grade levels, 131
    communicating with the community, 119–127
    deepening understanding with writing and reading, 61–88
    encouraging academic success, 11–25
    frequently asked questions, 131–137
    making space for speaking and listening, 39–59
    resistance, 12–13
    supporting personal growth, 27–38
    vs. traditional teaching approach, 131
supporting personal growth, 27–28
    imaginative freedom, 31–34
    independent thinking, 28–31
    integrity, 34–37
    next steps, 38

SurveyMonkey, 74
surveys, 72–75
    guidelines, 74–75

T

teacher's evaluation process explanation, 106
teacher-directed approach, 13–15
Teachers Going Gradeless blog, 121
text-based discussions, 84–87
    guidelines, 85–86
text-based seminars. *See* group work
The Things They Carried (O'Brien), 29, 45
third-person point of view, 77
This Is How We Do It (Lamothe), 63
Thompson-Grove, G., 84
Thoreau, H. D., 11
Three Minute Thesis, 53
timing of a speech, 54–56
Tomlinson, C. A., 101
totality of a student's work, 96
traditional grading systems, 89–94, 132
    myths about, 92
    vs. student-centered approach, 133
traditional teaching vs. student-centered learning, 131
Transforming Classroom Grading (Marzano), 97, 116
Treisman, U., 17–18

U

Understanding by Design (Wiggins & McTighe), 24
The Universal Schoolhouse (Moffett), 27
University of California, Berkeley, 41
    Bay Area Writing Project Summer Open Program, 19, 68
University of Connecticut, 122
University of Queensland, 53–54
us or them vs. all of us, 29

W

Wagner, B. J., 18, 27, 61, 94–96, 119, 129, 132
walk-in freezer, 122
Wall Street Journal, 36
"what if" questions, 38

Whitman, W., 82–83
Wiggins, G., 24
William Frantz Elementary School (New Orleans, La.), 3, 82
Wolfe, T., 75
worksheet for paired interviews, 42
Wormeli, R., 94
"A Writing Assignment / A Way of Life" (Martin, 48–49
writing, 9
    citing sources, 65–66
    deepening understanding with, 61–62
    field research, 68–77
    flexible dates and assessment, 49–50
    format, 66–68
    guidelines, 50
    Hallmark Factory, 41
    letters to the editor, 78–79
    next steps, 88
    occasional papers, 48–49
    process, 63–64
    provisional, 62–63
    research narratives, 62–68
    staying on topic, 52
    taking risks, 52
    with students, 51

Loving What They Learn
Alexander McNeece
Deep learning and high engagement are possible for all students, regardless of subject, grade, or previous experience. With *Loving What They Learn*, you will discover how to quantifiably measure students' needs, help strengthen their academic self-concept, and increase their self-efficacy.
BKF917

Ready to Learn
Peg Grafwallner
Ready to Learn introduces the FRAME model, a teacher-approved approach for creating meaningful and motivating learning experiences for all students. Rely on the model's five steps to help you launch engaging lessons, articulate clear expectations, and offer effective feedback.
BKF922

Standards-Based Learning in Action
Tom Schimmer, Garnet Hillman, and Mandy Stalets
Get past the knowing-doing gap and confidently implement standards-based learning in your classroom, school, or district. Each chapter offers readers a well-thought-out action plan for implementation and effective communication strategies for getting student and parent buy-in.
BKF782

Fifty Strategies to Boost Cognitive Engagement
Rebecca Stobaugh
Transform your classroom from one of passive knowledge consumption to one of active engagement. In this well-researched book, Rebecca Stobaugh shares 50 strategies for building a thinking culture that emphasizes essential 21st century skills—from critical thinking and problem-solving to teamwork and creativity.
BKF894

Visit SolutionTree.com or call 800.733.6786 to order.

"Tremendous, tremendous, tremendous!

The speaker made me do some very deep internal reflection about the **PLC process** and the personal responsibility I have in making the school improvement process work **for ALL kids**."

—Marc Rodriguez, teacher effectiveness coach, Denver Public Schools, Colorado

PD Services

Our experts draw from decades of research and their own experiences to bring you practical strategies for building and sustaining a high-performing PLC. You can choose from a range of customizable services, from a one-day overview to a multiyear process.

Book your PLC PD today!
888.763.9045

Solution Tree